CARS on Road & Track

BY JULIO TOLEDO DEL VALLE

A 29 2

STERLING PUBLISHING CO., INC.   NEW YORK

Oak Tree Press Co., Ltd.
London & Sydney

OTHER BOOKS OF INTEREST

Graham Hill's Car Racing Guide
Easy Motorcycle Riding
Bike-Ways (101 Things to Do with a Bike)
Safe Snowmobiling

Willers Overland 17 HP (1917)

Copyright © 1972 by Sterling Publishing Co., Inc.
419 Park Avenue South, New York, N.Y. 10016
This book was originally published under the title "el Automovil y su mundo," © 1968 by Santillana, S. A. de Ediciones Elfo, Madrid.
Translated by Natalia Garcia-Pardo
British edition published by Oak Tree Press Co., Ltd., Nassau, Bahamas
Distributed in Australia by Oak Tree Press Co., Ltd.,
P.O. Box 34, Brickfield Hill, Sydney 2000, N.S.W.
Distributed in the United Kingdom and elsewhere in the British Commonwealth
by Ward Lock Ltd., 116 Baker Street, London W 1
Manufactured in the United States of America   *All rights reserve*
Library of Congress Catalog Card No.: 71 167673
ISBN 0-8069-4046-8   UK 7061 2334-4
4047-6

Chevrolet 17 HP (1915)

CONTENTS

Introduction 5

A Brief History of the Automobile 6
    The Forerunners . . . The Development of Racing

Faster, Faster: The Battle for the Speed Record . . 19

Competition Cars 26
    The Different Groups . . . The Kart

The Engine 32
    Number and Placement of the Cylinders . . . Two- and Four-Stroke Engines . . . The Wankel Rotary Engine . . . Engine Placement . . . Measurements of the Power of the Engine

Anatomy of the Engine 40
    The Carburetor . . . Fuel Injection . . . Superchargers . . . The Valves . . . Ignition . . . Lubrication . . . The Cooling System . . . The Clutch

Transmission, Steering and Brakes 49
    The Transmission . . . The Differential . . . The Brakes . . . Steering

Chassis and Body 54
    The Chassis . . . The Body . . . Suspension

The Most Famous Cars 60
    Brabham . . . BRM . . . Chaparral . . . Cooper . . . Eagle . . . ERA . . . Ferrari . . . Ford . . . Jaguar . . . Lotus . . . March . . . McLaren . . . Mercedes-Benz . . . Porsche

Sports Trials 76
    Rallies . . . Hill Climbs . . . Speed Races

The Most Famous Races 86
    World Championship of Drivers

The Drivers 93

The Most Famous Circuits 101
    Avus . . . Brands Hatch . . . Le Mans . . . Monaco . . . Monza . . .
    Nurburgring . . . Sebring . . . Spa-Francorchamps

Index 112

The winner of the 1966 Italian Grand Prix at Monza, Ludovico Scarfiotti, races to the finish line.

INTRODUCTION

This book is not a manual to teach you how to drive, nor an intensive course in auto mechanics, nor a detailed listing of racing events. Instead, the goal here has been to present the car world to those who are interested—and to those who want to understand what all the excitement in racing is about!

Beginning with a concise history of the invention of the automobile, this book jumps into the fight for speed records by reporting the most famous races and their winners. Next comes a quick run-through of the parts of a car and how they work, in simple, easy-to-understand terms. And finally, a description of the sport of auto racing—the different types of competition cars and races, the tracks and events that are considered the most outstanding.

If you want to learn more about cars, racing and the excitement that is a natural part of it all—read on. You're sure to become enthused.

A BRIEF HISTORY OF THE AUTOMOBILE

THE FORERUNNERS

It is difficult to decide just which was the very first vehicle to be moved by its own energy—that is, an automobile (which means, literally, self moving)—although we can find vaguely related forerunners such as sailing ships on wheels that used the wind to propel them over land. But the first vehicle to move by its own energy was probably a model built between 1665 and 1680 by Father Ferdinand Verbiest, a Jesuit living in China. This first automobile was really a forerunner of today's turbine cars, since steam, generated by a fire in a round boiler, was not used directly but moved a horizontal turbine. By means of a simple system of gears, the steam energy made the wheels move.

A French military engineer, Nicholas Joseph Cugnot, built a tremendous tractor designed to pull artillery. Driven by a single person, this monster made its first journey in 1771 between Paris and Vincennes, France. Along the way, it knocked down a wall. The greatest importance of Cugnot's vehicle was that it showed the possibility of using steam engines (with pistons, not turbines) instead of horses.

While Cugnot's tractor went only 2.4 miles per hour, various improvements to the steam engine brought the speed up to 12 mph, reached in 1828 by W. H. James, an Englishman, in a steam carriage with 18 seats. In France, Amédée Bollée won special fame with his 12-passenger carriage, "L'Obeissante" (the "obedient one"), which in 1873 covered the route from Le Mans to Paris at an average speed of 25.2 mph, and violated the law 75 times in the course of the trip! As you can see, traffic violations are as old as the car itself.

A stagecoach with a steam engine. Steam, made by boiling water in the large barrel, moved other parts and finally the wheels.

Motors were powered by other things besides steam. Electric power seemed to offer new potential when, in 1882, an Englishman named Ayrton invented the first practical electric car. In 1889 the Belgian Camille Jenatzy built his "La Jamais Contente," an extraordinary electric car that was to set a speed record in 1899 of 65.79 mph. The car is noteworthy for having exceeded the 60 mph mark and for being one of the first automobiles with an aerodynamic shape—this in an age when car bodies were similar to horse-drawn buggies! Ferdinand Porsche, whose name is associated now with magnificent sports cars, made himself famous with the success of his 12-horsepower electric vehicles. Their cleanliness and silent operation were offset, however, by the limited distance they could travel—only 30 to 60 miles. The electric motor was soon dominated by the more advanced com-

The Daimler motor car next to a picture of its inventor, Gottlieb Daimler. This car is preserved in the Munich Museum.

One of the first "automobiles" was no more than a motor mounted on the back of a bicycle, with small wheels in the back for balance. This example is Gottlieb Daimler's model.

bustion engines, but the idea of the electric motor has endured and may even have a great future.

Although we have talked about the electric motor before the internal combustion engine, this is not the true sequence, since the latter is the older and more important of the two. Between 1890 and 1900, there was an enormous increase in the number of cars with internal combustion engines. One of the oldest is the Austrian Markus, now in the Technical Museum of Vienna.

The internal combustion engine itself, however, had already been invented some time before this. Among the earlier engines, one by the French-Belgian Jean Joseph Etienne Lenoir is remarkable for being among the first to burn gasoline and for being produced in quantity—some 400 were made. But the title "father of the internal combustion engine" is usually given to the German Nicholas August Otto. After many ups and downs, he became manager of the Deutz Motor Factory. When Otto arrived on the scene Deutz motors were heavy and had limited power, and so were not suitable for automobiles. Of the two

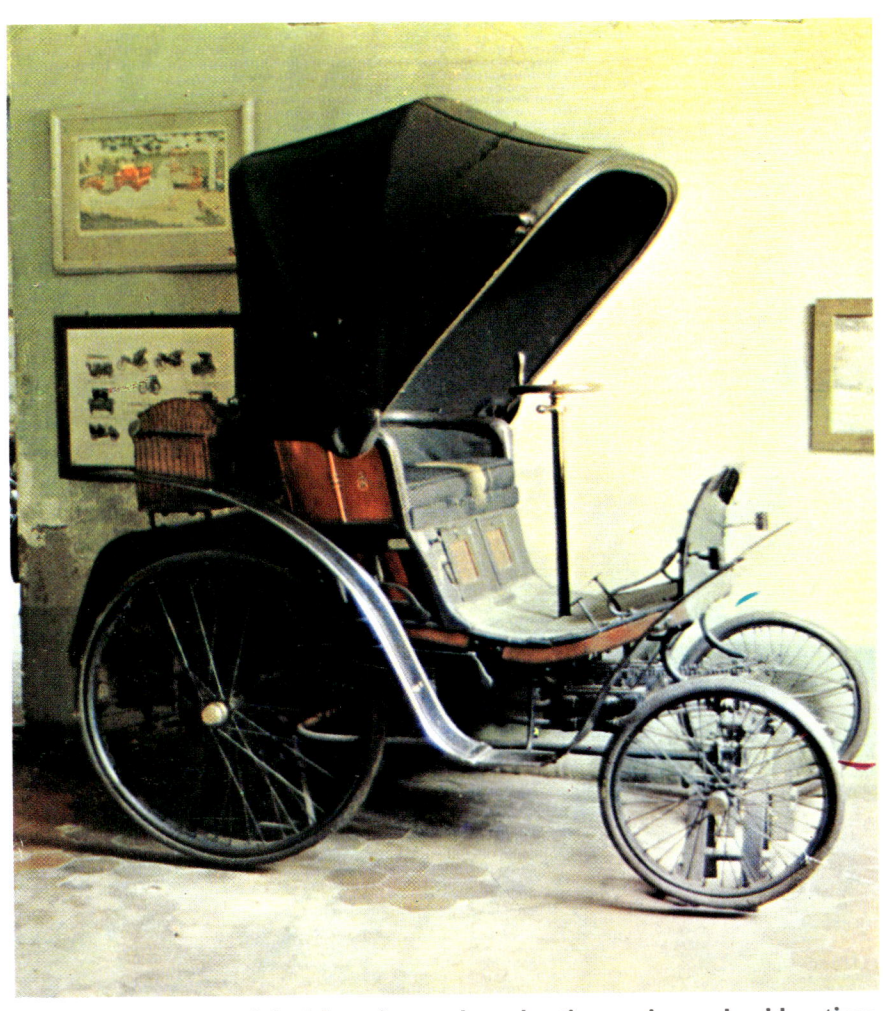

An early model with an internal combustion engine and rubber tires.

models manufactured, one weighed 1,320 pounds but produced only one half a horsepower; the other weighed 3,454 pounds and produced two horsepower. Otto improved the motor by developing what was to become the classic four-stroke engine. Unfortunately, the fight for patents and the lawsuits which resulted hastened the death of this jovial inventor in 1891.

A major advance in the development of the primitive motor was due to Wilhelm Maybach who invented a motor to run on gasoline instead of illuminating gas. Gottlieb Daimler, who had been with the Deutz factory but left in 1882 after internal disputes, associated himself with Maybach to design a lighter, more powerful engine that could move a coach. They succeeded in 1884, and the motor is preserved today in the Munich Museum. They reduced 1,620 lbs. of engine to 88 lbs. for one horsepower. The automobile engine as we know it today was born.

    Daimler first mounted the engine on a reinforced bicycle, a sort of motorcycle, and equipped it with some small auxiliary side wheels for its public appearance on November 10, 1885. This unexpected sight shocked the first witnesses of progress. He built his first car the following year. Like the early efforts of other pioneer builders, Daimler's version was nothing more than a horse-drawn carriage with the horses replaced by a motor that occupied part of the floor near the rear seats.

    Daimler was a great motor enthusiast: he also added motors to

A picture of Carl Benz next to his 1886 invention, the three-wheeled Benz-Dreirad.

a boat and a balloon, thereby extending motorization—however rudimentary—to transportation by land, sea and air. In the famous Paris Exposition of 1889 for which the Eiffel Tower was erected, Daimler, in collaboration with Maybach, presented a steel automobile with a new motor which had the cylinders arranged in a V. This was no longer an experimental motor mounted on a carriage meant for horses, but a coach of metal construction, a proper automobile constructed of steel and, like the Eiffel Tower, a symbol of things to come.

The presentation in Paris was a success and marked the starting point for French automobiles. Among the early French cars, those made by Emile Levassor and René Panhard stand out. Panhard's name is honored even today on a make of car. On the Panhard-Levassor were more improvements: the motor enclosed in a hood up front, wheels with rubber tires, and a chain-driven transmission with a three-speed gearbox. The motor had two cylinders with a displacement, or cylinder capacity, of 74.42 cu. in. (1,220 cc), producing four horsepower at 800 rpm with a top speed of 18.6 mph. (If you are unfamiliar with these terms, see pages 32 to 39.) The automobile was beginning to assume its true form. At this time Peugeot produced a curious car with four seats placed face to face. It was powered by a 36.6 cu. in. (600 cc) Daimler engine, a size popular in Europe now, producing four horsepower and a speed of 9.6 mph.

The number of automobiles increased and within seven years of the Exposition, there were already 500 cars in Paris. At the same time, the first traffic problems arose as pedestrians and policemen were pushed off the road by those crazy motorists.

Nothing was easy in those years. The early automobile men encountered every kind of difficulty and lack of understanding. Establishing patents produced long law suits that ruined these men both spiritually and materially. As with Otto, financial difficulties embittered the last years of Panhard's life and he lived only three months into the new century. Benz, who invented the two-stroke engine and whose experiments were similar to those of Daimler, also passed through very difficult economic situations. And the incomprehension and annoyance of the public and the authorities added to the inventors' difficulties. The automobile's first appearances took place, for the most part, with an indignant audience looking on from the sidewalks and horse-drawn carriages. The authorities set ridiculous prohibitions on traffic

Shown in the racing department of the Daimler-Benz Museum is the "Blitzen-Benz," or "Lightning Benz," of 1911.

which, while creating difficulties for these spirited men, did not stop them from pursuing their efforts to improve the automobile.

The taxes and fees that burden car owners today are not modern inventions either. Two years before the end of the 19th century, taxes of 6 francs were levied on single-seater cars, 12 francs on those with two seats and 18 francs on those with three. The same thing happened to license plates: fees varied according to where the car was owned and the number of seats it had, ranging from 110 francs in Paris for cars with more than two seats to 25 francs in cities with a population of less than 10,000 for cars with only one or two seats.

In addition to Daimler and Benz in Germany and Panhard-Levassor, Peugeot, De Dion Bouton, Bollée and Renault in France, other pioneer inventors were Ford, Packard and Stanley in the United States, Lanchester and Knight in England, and Fiat and Lanza in Italy. In some cases, the names of the early automobile makers are still used as names of cars manufactured today.

Renault (1905)

Ford Model T (1919)

Further improvements were made not only to the engines (resulting in lighter weight but greater power) but also to basic parts such as the ignition. In the earliest gasoline motors, the gaseous mixture was ignited by means of an actual flame. Daimler improved this rudimentary system somewhat by using a small incandescent tube, but he could not get rid of the dangerous flame. In 1884, Otto used an electromagnetic ignition. Benz made even more improvements, but Robert Bosch invented ignition by magneto, a system that served for forty years until it was replaced by the present battery system. Bosch's name is still well-known as the trademark of a battery manufacturing firm.

THE DEVELOPMENT OF RACING

Racing, which is the butt of many unfavorable comments yet still has many enthusiastic fans, encouraged the technical perfection of the automobile. In December, 1893, a Parisian newspaper announced that a race would be run the following spring between Paris and Rouen. Over 100 people applied, and 21 were selected to race. The 75.6 miles were covered in only 5 hours and 40 minutes by a De Dion steam car driven by De Dion's associate, Bouton. Of the competing cars, 15 finished, making the occasion

A set of tires can win or lose a race. Every time a car races, it uses a new set.

a genuine success not only as a sporting event but as a demonstration of the possibilities of this new-fangled horseless carriage.

The first long race took place on June 11, 1895 from Paris to Bordeaux and back to Paris (732 miles). Of the 21 participants, sportsman-builder Emile Levassor was the first to arrive at Bordeaux—only to find that they had not expected any contestants until much later! Levassor returned to Paris, completing the race in 48 hours and 47 minutes for an average speed of 15.01 mph. From this race De Dion concluded that the steam engine could no longer compete with the combustion engine, so he turned to building the latter. This race gave the automobile an important boost, as its publicity acquainted people with cars and increased their sales. Also, on the initiative of Count De Dion, the Automobile Club of France was founded in the same year. This organization was very influential in developing racing as a sport.

At the beginning of the 20th century, the automobile had passed out of its first phase, invention, into a second phase, that of industrial manufacturing. Germany, Austria, The United States, England, Italy and France had factories for auto production.

Although we have already spoken of the development of the motor and the ignition, we certainly cannot fail to mention something as important as the wheel—one of the most basic inventions which did not change for centuries, until the appearance of the horseless carriage. On the first cars, the wheels were exactly like those on the horse-drawn carriages of the age—wood with a metal tire. The cars displayed at the Paris Exposition of 1889 were improved somewhat by having steel wheels. Solid rubber tires were added later, and finally pneumatic or air-filled rubber tires were used. This last development was due to a Scotsman, John Boyd Dunlop, who first put them on bicycles. A large part of the credit for greater speed—and also for greater safety—goes to Dr. Dunlop, whose name still stands in the automobile industry on one of the principal brands of tires.

In discussing the huge growth of the automobile industry, we cannot leave out the United States. The American industry was held back at first by a patent registered by lawyer George Selden. The first truly American car was the Duryea, built in 1893, which was the winner of the Chicago race of 1895. The first American car produced in quantity was the 1900 Oldsmobile "Curved Dash," a two-seater powered by a single horizontal cylinder and

The race begins! Hunched low in their seats, the drivers use their wits and depend on perfectly tuned engines to forge ahead.

a water-cooled 7-horsepower engine, with two forward gears and a top speed of 18 mph. These were built over a period of three years in Detroit, Michigan—what was to become the car capital of America.

Even in this short history of the automobile, the fabulous Henry Ford must be mentioned. Although he was not the builder of the first American car nor the founder of the industry, he is a legendary figure whose name has endured on his car. Ford cars have gained prestige not only as regular production models but also in sports cars, in Europe as well as in America. Ford cars have won several recent runnings of the most famous test in the world, *Les Vingt-Quatre Heures du Mans*, or the Le Mans 24 Hours. The most famous Ford model was the "T," produced from October, 1908 until April, 1927. In all, 15,000,000 Model T's were produced. Instead of having his workmen build one car at a time, Ford placed them in a row so that each man performed a particular task as the cars moved down the assembly line. With mass production, Ford succeeded in turning out a car every 40 seconds, drastically lowering its price and thus making the car available to many people.

FASTER, FASTER: THE BATTLE FOR THE SPEED RECORD

The competition to establish an automobile speed record began on December 18, 1898 in Acheres, France and has not stopped since. The first mark of 39.24 mph was set by Count Gaston de Chasseloup-Laubat in a 36-hp. electric car that weighed 3,080 lbs. Not even a month later, the Belgian engineer Camille Jenatzy appeared in Acheres with a different electric car and reached a speed of 41.33 mph. This was on the morning of January 17, 1899 and on that very same afternoon, Count Chasseloup-Laubat raised the record again to 43.59 mph. From that day the battle for the speed record became a duel between the French count and the Belgian engineer. On January 27 the record passed again to Jenatzy at 49.79 mph, with Chasseloup-Laubat raising it on March 4 to 58.09 mph. The top mark finally went to the Belgian on April 29 at 65.65 mph with his aerodynamic "La Jamais Contente"—and all this in only 1899!

But this record did not last very long either. Other kinds of engines were threatening the electric ones, but it was still not the gasoline engine that took the title next. Instead, a steam engine car, driven by Leon Serpallet, reached 74.90 mph in Nice on April 13, 1902. Weighing 3,960 lbs., the car had 106 horsepower.

The Mors, a very famous French sports car in those days, set three records in 1902, on August 5, November 5 and November 17, driven by W. K. Vanderbilt, Henry Fournier and Augieres. The greatest speed was 76.96 mph. The Mors had a four-cylinder internal combustion engine with a displacement of 563 cu. in., giving 60 horsepower.

In Ostende on July 15, 1903, a Gobron-Brille car that already looked like a modern racing machine reached 84.51 mph. Driven by Arthur Duray, this vehicle had 100 horsepower with a displacement of 823.5 cu. in. (13,500 cc), a tubular chassis and four forward gears. Its weight was only 2,189 lbs.

Americans entered the competition with as famous a car as a Ford, the well-known 999 with a 1,019 cu. in. (16,708 cc)

Car after car after car is lined up in front of the stands for a last-minute check before a modern-day race.

cylinder capacity and 72 horsepower. This tremendous monster, with no gearshift or differential (see page 50), seemed a jump backwards compared to the modern-looking Gobron-Brille. Nevertheless, the car exceeded the old record by reaching 91 mph, but this was not officially recognized.

Another glorious name, Mercedes, went 92.1 mph in Daytona, Florida on January 28, 1904. Driven by W. K. Vanderbilt, this car had a 530.7 cu. in. (8,700 cc), four-cylinder engine of 90 horsepower.

In Europe again, a Gobron-Brille regained the speed record, driven this time by Louis Emile Rigolly. On March 31, 1904, in Nice, a new model with some changes in the body shape and an increase of 10 horsepower in the engine brought the record to 94.6 mph.

Ostende was the scene next, where a Mercedes driven by Baron Caters reached 97.0 mph. His car had less power and a smaller displacement than that of Rigolly who, on the same site two months later, reached 103.2 mph with his Gobron-Brille. At the end of 1904, a Darracq driven in Ostende by P. Baras raised the record to 104.3 mph.

The English also entered the competition, but on American soil, on January 24, 1905. A. McDonald made 104.3 mph in Daytona with a Napier car of 911 cu. in. (14,934 cc) displacement, 90 horsepower and three forward gears.

Victor Hemery reached 109.1 mph on December 30, 1905, in a Darracq with four cylinders placed in a V. The engine displacement was a gigantic 1,373.6 cu. in. (22,518 cc), producing 200 horsepower.

A surprising event occurred in 1906 when, several years after the internal combustion engine had been accepted as the best, a steam car set a new record. Frank Marriot raised the mark in a Stanley Steamer to 121.30 mph in Daytona on January 26th. This Stanley was a curiosity in aerodynamics: it had a wooden body and only a 50-horsepower engine.

Four years passed before the Stanley's record was broken. Barney Oldfield brought his 1,311.5 cu. in. (21,500 cc), 200-horsepower Benz to Daytona, running it at 131 mph, but his speed was not officially approved.

Four years later, L. G. Hornsted established a new official mark of 123 mph in Brooklands, England with another Benz. Then racing took a long time-out, due to World War I and its after-effects. The 124-mph mark was officially broken on May 17, 1922 when K. L. Guinness, driving a Sunbeam at Brooklands, was recorded at 128 mph. His Sunbeam was powered by a V-12 airplane engine which had 1,117.6 cu. in. (18,322 cc) and 350 horsepower.

On September 25, 1924, the name Campbell entered the record books for the first time. A great deal was heard of this name in later years, spanning two generations of Campbells. Malcolm Campbell set his first mark on September 25, 1924 in Pendine, driving a Sunbeam equipped with a 350-horsepower V-12 airplane engine of 1,117.6 cu. in. (18,322 cc). On July 21, 1925 he raised the record to 150 mph with the same car.

On March 16, 1926, Sir Henry Seagrave reached a speed of 151 mph with another Sunbeam of 242.5 cu. in. (3,976 cc) and 306 horsepower with a compressor-supercharger (a "souped up" engine). In the same year, J. P. G. Thomas raised the mark twice with a Higham V-12 Liberty airplane motor of 500 horsepower and 1,641.3 cu. in. (26,907 cc). Weighing 4,400 lbs., his vehicle reached 170 mph on April 29th.

Malcolm Campbell returned with a Napier-Campbell, again equipped with an airplane engine—this one 502 horsepower. In Pendine, the fashionable place for races in those days, he achieved 174.46 mph on February 2, 1927. On March 29th, his competitor Seagrave got his car up to 203.29 mph at Daytona. Seagrave had equipped his Sunbeam with *two* airplane engines, which produced a total of 1,000 hp. with a displacement of 2,737.7 cu. in. (44,880 cc).

A car as fast as a comet races alongside the protective guard rails.

Crowds strain forward to see the Le Mans 24 Hours.

Over 200 mph! This was a difficult record to break, and Campbell did not succeed in doing so until February 19, 1928. In Daytona, his blue Napier-Campbell racer, very streamlined but less powerful than Seagrave's car, raised the mark to 213 mph. Two months later, Ray Keech appeared on the scene with a White Triplex fitted with *three* 500-hp. Liberty motors and promptly nudged the record up to a new high of 213.3 mph.

The next year, 1929, Seagrave brought the Irving Special to Daytona. Speeding across the smooth, flat sands, he pushed the record to 230.88 mph. Meanwhile, Malcolm Campbell had substantially changed his Napier-Campbell. In Daytona, on February 5th, 1931, he broke the 240-mph-barrier by establishing a speed of 249.9 mph. His "Bluebird," the name he gave to his car, was 24′ 7″ long and weighed 6,600 lbs. The Napier engine with a centrifugal supercharger produced 1,350 hp. In February of the following year, still in Daytona, the same car made the incredible speed of 253.35 mph.

23

Campbell, in an untiring pursuit of speed, changed the Napier engine for a supercharged Rolls-Royce R. With a displacement of 2,227.9 cu. in. (36,523 cc), the new engine produced 2,500 hp. at 3,200 rpm. Body modifications made the Bluebird even more streamlined, and at the Bonneville Salt Flats in Utah, Campbell boosted the record to 300.46 mph on February 22, 1933.

In the years before World War II, two more drivers entered their names in the record books. In 1937 and 1938, George Eyston in his "Thunderbolt" not only crossed the 350-mph-barrier, but even raised the record to 356.63 mph. Weighing 15,400 lbs., his car was powered by two supercharged Rolls-Royce engines producing 5,000 hp.

Eyston's record, set in August, 1938, was threatened on September 15 by John Cobb's Napier-Railton with two supercharged Napier "lion" engines of 2,500 hp. each. With traction on all four wheels, Cobb's car was clocked at 347 mph, and 354 mph on the following day. The record, however, remained with Eyston until the next year. On August 23rd, 1939, just days before World War II began in Europe, the record went to Cobb at 368.81 mph. In 1947, John Cobb came back to Bonneville with the Napier-Railton and on September 16th set a new high mark of 393.33 mph.

Among the technical advances to come out of the war were turbine engines, which later gave tremendous power to racing cars. Donald Campbell—the second generation of this name in the sporting world—constructed another Bluebird, this one moved by a 5,000-hp. turbine engine. On July 17, 1964, across the bed of dry Lake Eyre in Australia, the new Bluebird was clocked at 402.21 mph.

Classification became somewhat complicated with the appearance of cars, both piston and turbine, which are powered like jets, with direct transmission of power to the wheels. Some of these new cars have only three wheels on the ground instead of four. Instead of one record for all cars, several categories were established in 1965. The present holders of the records are:

For automobiles with four wheels with power transmission to two, equipped with two or more motors—Bob Summers, U.S.A., "Goldenrod," 406.50 mph.

For turbine cars with four wheels with power transmission to two, equipped with two or more motors—Donald Campbell, Great Britain, "Bluebird II," 402.24 mph.

An accident on the track is not uncommon. Both driver and car must be removed from the track immediately to prevent other cars from crashing into the debris.

For vehicles with three wheels, unrestricted propulsion (Motorcycle Federation category)—Craig Breedlove, U.S.A., "Spirit of America," 525.45 mph.

For special vehicles with four wheels, unrestricted propulsion —the absolute record holder, Craig Breedlove, U.S.A., with his "Spirit of America—Sonic I," 600.601 mph.

COMPETITION CARS

All cars have the same parts that are described later, but competition cars demand special attention and, frequently, special parts. Races have been lost because of one slightly maladjusted part—so infinite care is taken in preparing a racing machine.

The principal automotive sports organizations have established a series of categories that includes the whole range of automobiles, from the point of view of competition cars. The following is only a brief introduction; if you are interested in acquainting yourself thoroughly with this system of regulations, the Federation Internationale de l'Automobile (FIA), the Paris-based world governing body of auto racing, can supply you with complete and proper rules.

THE DIFFERENT GROUPS

The purpose of establishing separate groups of cars is so cars of equal weights, displacements and other specifications race together. The FIA regulations which establish these groups and formulas challenge designers to create more efficient machines within the limitations imposed on them. It is not difficult to design a car that goes fast if there are no limitations as to engine size or anything else. But the challenge of designing a fast-moving car within certain limitations calls on the skills of the designer and the driver, particularly on circuits with tortuous curves and climbs. The regulations make auto racing a true sport.

GROUP 1. This is also known as STANDARD TOURING, grouping together those cars of which at least 5,000 were built in 12 consecutive months. In this group, and for cars with a displacement greater than 42.7 cu. in. (700 cc), the cars must have four seats. They must be strictly standard make and not have undergone any modification or special preparation that betters their performance. Only a few small modifications are authorized. What is intended with this group is to use ordinary cars in competition, for those people who are sports car fans but do not have the money to buy special racing cars.

GROUP 2. TOURING. This category applies to cars of a more limited series—1,000 as the minimum production in one year. In this group some transformations are authorized, with the object of making the cars more fit for competition. Cars classified in Group 1 are also included, but can use the modifications that are authorized for Group 2, such as changes in the engine, carburetor, muffler, and other places.

A completed car being towed onto the track. Every part of the car is examined before it rolls by its own power.

GROUP 3. GRAND TOURING. This group consists of high performance cars manufactured in an even more limited series—500 in 12 consecutive months. By contrast with the first two groups, two-seaters are allowed, with any displacement. The same modifications as in Group 2 are permitted.

GROUP 4. SPORTS. These are high performance cars whose production is limited to only 50 examples in the regulation 12 months. They can be two-seaters, but they must have all the elements required for vehicles that travel on public roads. There are a number of regulations with which the 50 production examples must conform. There is a minimum weight in relation to the displacement, ranging from 990 lbs. for displacements of less than 30.5 cu. in. (500 cc), up to 1,650 lbs. for those of more than 305 cu. in. (5,000 cc).

GROUP 5. SPECIAL TOURING. These are cars of Groups 1 and 2 which, while keeping the original body, have undergone certain transformations that exclude them from the other groups.

GROUP 6. SPORTS-PROTOTYPE. These cars are manufactured especially for speed or endurance races, where certain specifications of outfitting and equipment are established.

GROUP 7. TWO-SEATER RACING. These are two-seater competition cars, conceived and manufactured exclusively for speed trials in a closed circuit. In Europe they usually only participate in hill climbs.

Some series are established according to number of cylinders and their displacement. The limitations put on these cars are very few, such as the use of commercial fuel, starting the motor inside the car, stop lights, and using headlights only in night trials. The use of safety devices is obligatory, such as seat belts for the driver, fire walls between the engine and the seat, fire extinguishers, roll bars over the top of the car, and other items designed to protect the driver.

GROUP 8. SINGLE-SEATER RACING:

Formula 1. The actual formula, or specifications, for this group will be in effect from January, 1966 to December 31, 1972. (Formulas are revised approximately every six years by the FIA.) The displacement without supercharging must be equal to or less than 183 cu. in. (3,000 cc). The use of the rotary piston engine and gas turbine is permitted, as long as the equivalent of the authorized displacement is not exceeded. The minimum weight for a car is 1,073 lbs. Commercial gasoline must be used.

If an open racing car overturns, the roll bar situated above and behind the driver protects him from being pinned or crushed under his car.

Formula 2. This formula is in effect between January 1, 1967 and December 31, 1971. Engines must have no more than six cylinders, with a displacement between 79.3 and 97.6 cu. in. (1,300 and 1,600 cc). The minimum weight is 934 lbs. The cylinder block must come from a car with a minimum production of 500 in 12 months. Neither supercharging nor traction with more than two wheels is permitted.

Formula 3. This formula began on January 1, 1964 and is scheduled to be changed in December, 1971 to a displacement of 97.6 cu. in. (1,600 cc). The engine of alternating pistons, currently with a maximum displacement of 61 cu. in. (1,000 cc), must not have more than four cylinders, must be obtained from a mass-produced automobile manufactured in a minimum number of 1,000 in 12 months, and must be sanctioned by the FIA. Engines with overhead camshafts are excluded. Limitations are also established on the carburetor, transmission, and other things. Maximum weight is 880 lbs.

GROUP 9. OTHER SINGLE-SEATERS. In this group are the rest of the single-seaters which are not defined in the three previous formulas, including Formula 4, Formula V (the initial of Volkswagen, whose basic parts are used), nationals, etc. This group makes competitive racing available to a large number of amateurs who cannot spend a lot of money on their cars.

This is the classification of cars of the Federation Internationale de l'Automobile (FIA). Not included are other types of sports cars, such as stock cars, dragsters, funny cars; the special types, such as midgets and variations; and many more, which we cannot discuss at length here.

Mechanics watch with interest as a racing car approaches the pits.

While karts are considerably smaller than other racing cars, they are still to be reckoned with. Fun to drive and inexpensive, karting has made it possible for anyone to race.

THE KART

The kart is the only competitive car which is truly accessible to anyone, with a good model costing less than $250. Invented in 1956 by a Californian named Art Ingels, the first kart was no more than a rectangle of tubing, with small scooter wheels on each corner and a 2.5 hp. engine in the back. This little model reached 30 mph.

As karts became popular, competition events were established. It was necessary to have regulations for karting events, and the International Kart Federation presently handles this. Not only are there different classifications for karts but also for drivers, depending on their age and weight (lightweight drivers would have an advantage over heavier ones if they raced together).

Karts are mainly for fun, but with the proper engine and track, they can reach some pretty serious speeds—100 mph is not uncommon. Naturally, strict safety regulations must be observed, since the driver is quite unprotected as he sits on the kart's little chassis.

THE ENGINE

The engine is the heart of the car. Men wanted to replace the horse with something inside the car that would move the wheels. In one of the first cars, a steam engine was used, but today this is strictly a relic of the past. The electric motor, while used only occasionally, has not been completely forgotten. It is hoped that one day the technical problems—its heavy weight and the short life of the important batteries—will be overcome, giving electric cars enough range to make them really practical. The internal combustion engine was the best solution for the automobile. The turbine engine and the rotary engine are now being experimented with, but much remains to be done before they can be manufactured on a large scale.

NUMBER AND PLACEMENT OF THE CYLINDERS

The first internal combustion engine had just one cylinder. To increase its power, it was logical to increase the displacement—that is, the volume of the cylinder, filled with the gasoline/air mixture. With only one cylinder, however, this meant a too-large cylinder, as well as a jerky ride. So the next step was to increase the number of cylinders—from one to two, later to three, still later to four and even six. This made another difficulty—the need for a large space to house such a big motor. One solution was to arrange the cylinders in a V, an idea adopted by Daimler in 1889 and subsequently used on many cars with large displacements. The arrangement of the cylinders can be in a line, one behind the other, but this is usually not used for engines with more than four cylinders.

Other motors use still other arrangements—placing two cylinders horizontally and opposite one another, as in the well-known Citroen 2HP; four cylinders opposed two and two as in the Volkswagen; or even six cylinders opposed three and three as in the Porsche. The V arrangement is most common for eight or more cylinders.

The displacement is always given as part of the data of any car. The displacement—sometimes called the cylinder capacity—of an engine is found by first figuring the volume of each cylinder (multiply the area of the cylinder's base times its height) and then multiplying that number times the number of cylinders.

TWO- AND FOUR-STROKE ENGINES

The two-stroke engine is very simple, since the cylinders have no valves to admit the gas. Instead, the gaseous mixture enters and leaves the cylinders through openings that are covered and uncovered as the piston moves up and down. Oil to lubricate the pistons is mixed with the gasoline. Two-stroke engines are used in only a few cars (DKW and Saab, for example).

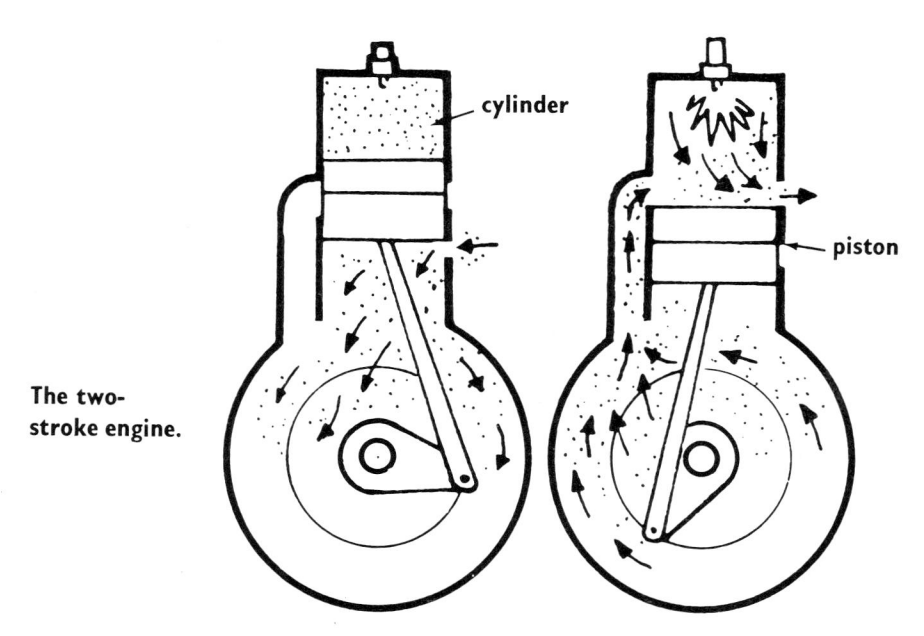

The two-stroke engine.

intake valve

cylinder

piston

intake stroke

compression stroke

exhaust valve

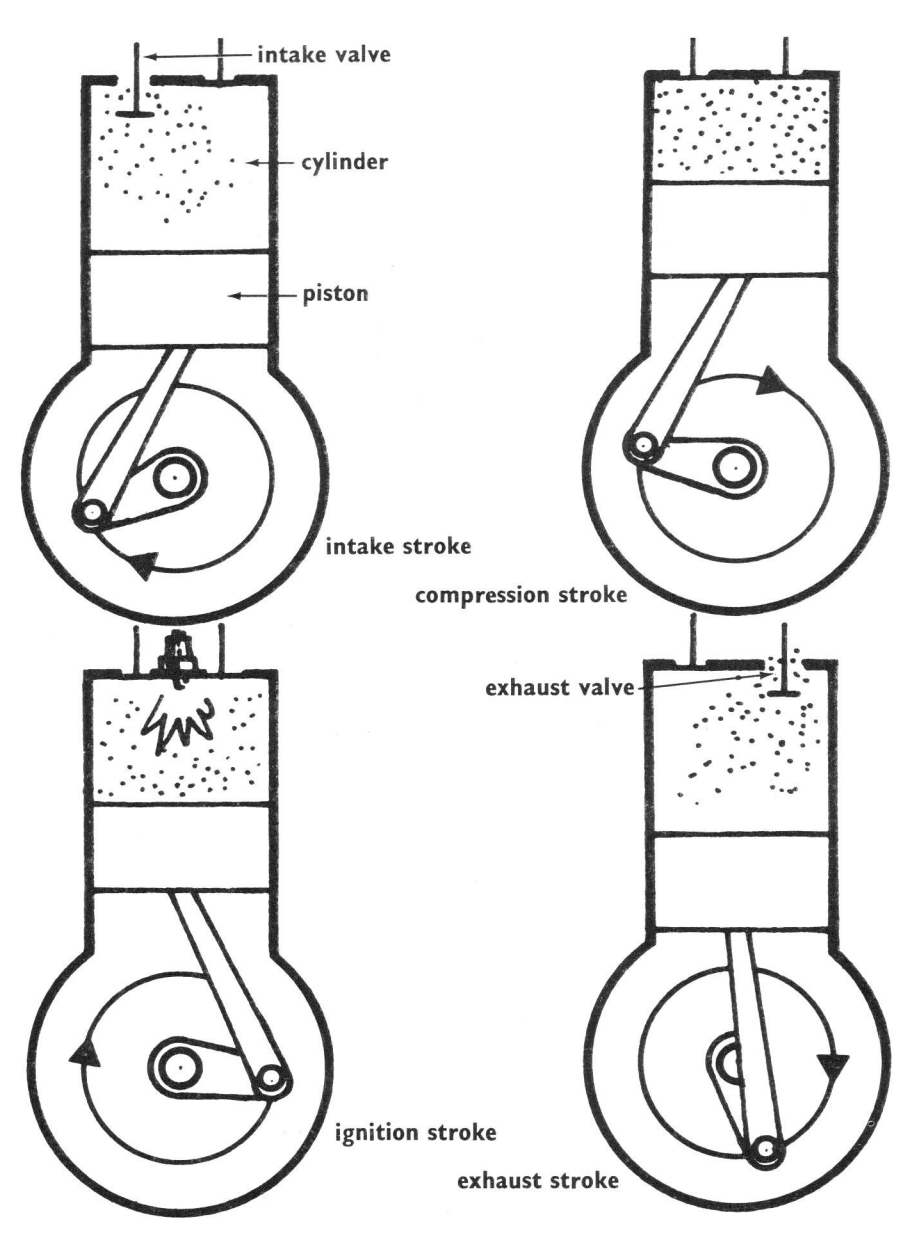

ignition stroke

exhaust stroke

In the first stroke, the intake valve opens to admit the gasoline/air mixture. In the second stroke, the mixture is compressed. The spark plug ignites the mixture, causing an explosion in the third stroke. Finally, the exhaust valve opens and the fumes leave the cylinder. Notice the position of the piston during each of the four strokes.

As the piston moves downward in a two-stroke engine, the two openings in the wall of the cylinder are uncovered and leftover gases leave through the escape vent. At the same time, fresh gases are drawn into the interior of the cylinder from the carburetor. As the piston moves upward, the gases are compressed until the spark plug ignites them, causing an explosion and sending the piston downward again.

In the four-stroke engine, the gases enter and leave the cylinders through valves. The gasoline/air mixture does not require oil since lubrication is provided in another way (see page 45). Every set of four strokes makes one revolution of the engine (*rpm* means the number of revolutions per minute).

First Stroke: INTAKE. The intake valve opens as the piston moves down, drawing a mixture of gasoline and air into the cylinder from the carburetor. The amount of gaseous mixture that each cylinder holds times the number of cylinders is the displacement.

Second Stroke: COMPRESSION. The intake valve closes as the piston moves up, compressing the gaseous mixture that fills the cylinder.

Third Stroke: IGNITION. As the piston nears the top of the cylinder, a spark from the spark plug causes the gaseous mixture to explode. This explosion forces the piston downward again.

Fourth Stroke: EXHAUST. The piston returns upwards as the exhaust valve opens. The remaining gas is forced out by the piston, completing the four-stroke sequence.

THE WANKEL ROTARY ENGINE

Another type of engine not yet manufactured for general use is the rotary engine, invented by Dr. Felix Wankel. It is much simpler, smaller and lighter than the four-stroke engine. Wankel's engine consists of a fixed cylinder with an interior chamber shaped like a figure eight with a thick waist, within which turns an equilateral triangle with curved sides. The points of the triangle are constantly in contact with the walls of the chamber. As the triangle turns in the figure eight, the sizes of the three chambers it forms vary, and the four-stroke sequence takes place as usual.

This motor, because it rotates and does not move up and down, reduces vibration considerably. Its main disadvantage is the lack of reserve power within its three chambers, resulting in greater wear and little breaking power from the motor. Work is currently being done to perfect this motor, as it offers a solution to pollutants from unburned gasoline.

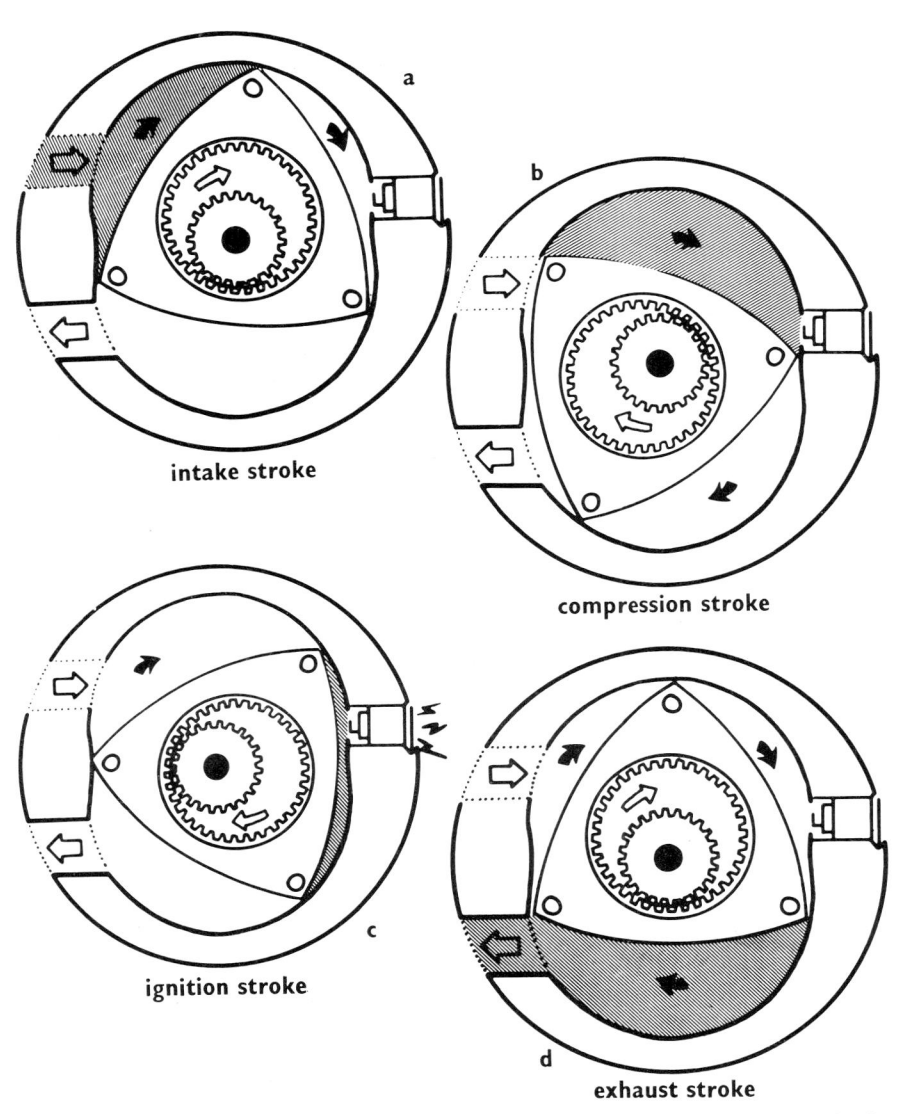

a intake stroke

b compression stroke

c ignition stroke

d exhaust stroke

The Wankel rotating motor. Notice that the only moving part is the triangle, forming chambers of different sizes. In c, the spark plug ignites, just as in the third stroke of a four-stroke cylinder engine.

ENGINE PLACEMENT

Before discussing the different elements that make up the engine, let us first see where the engine belongs. The classic arrangement has been to place the engine lengthwise in front of the car, with the transmission in the rear to provide motion. In general, the engine is placed vertically but it can be at an angle (as in the Citroen 2HP) to let the driver see over the hood more easily.

The most important reason for having the engine in the front is the possibility of front-wheel drive, where the front wheels provide both power and steering. The motor is sometimes placed sideways in cars which have front-wheel drive.

A car with the engine in front and the transmission in the rear has several advantages: the car is very stable, particularly when turning, braking and accelerating. Its main disadvantages are that the transmission takes up space on the floor of the car; the car has greater weight; and the rear wheels adhere poorly.

When a car has both the engine and transmission in front, it is still very stable. It is not affected by side winds and turns evenly and safely at normal speeds. It tends to swerve at high speeds, however, turn heavily at low speeds, and wear the front tires excessively when parking.

The practical cars produced just after World War II usually had the engine in the rear. In this arrangement, the engine is placed lengthwise in front of the rear axle (connected to the rear wheels), while the transmission is usually in front of the differential (a part connected to the rear axle—see page 50). The engine is usually vertical but it can also be horizontal, as it is in the Volkswagen.

By having both the motor and transmission in the rear, the car has good traction of the driving wheels. It steers easily and brakes well because the weight is well distributed. The body can be sleekly shaped, with no obstructions in front. One disadvantage is over-steering, although in certain circumstances such as racing this can be a plus factor, if the driver knows how to take advantage of it. The car is also susceptible to side winds, and poor cooling. There are difficulties in connecting the engine to the wheels.

The engine can also be placed in the center of the car, but this is used only for competition cars because it takes up useful space.

MEASUREMENTS OF THE POWER OF THE ENGINE

Discussing the horsepower of a car's engine is sometimes confusing, as there are several different figures that can be called "horsepower." The rated horsepower, sometimes called chevaux-vapeur (CV), indicates the effective power of a given engine. The taxable horsepower in most countries is calculated by means of a complicated formula whose real intention is to determine how much the car's license should cost. The rated horsepower is the real measure of an engine's power. One hp. is the equivalent of 550 foot-pounds per second—that is, the power necessary to raise 550 pounds of weight one foot in one second.

Once you realize this difference, however, figures about horsepower can still be confusing. There may be different figures for the rated horsepower of one car. This is because of the different methods of calculating horsepower, indicated by the initials DIN, SAE or CUNA. To express horsepower according to the DIN (Deutsche Industrie Normen) standard, the engine must be equipped with all the accessories normally attached in the car (generator, starter, filter, etc.) when the horsepower is calculated. The standards of the CUNA (Commissio Unificaziones Normalizazione Autovehicoli) allow the air filter and the muffler to be left off when the horsepower is figured. The SAE (Society of Automotive Engineers) standards permit not only the air filter and muffler to be detached, but also the generator, water pump, clutch and gasoline pump.

So one car can have 43 hp. DIN, 47 hp. CUNA and 51 hp. SAE! In advertising a car it is understood that manufacturers quote the large SAE figure, even though the DIN is more accurate.

The torque, or turning force, is expressed in foot-pounds. An engine that has a torque of 108 fp. means that its crankshaft force is the same as the force produced by 108 pounds hanging from the end of a one-foot-long horizontal shaft.

The power of an engine depends on the displacement of the cylinders and the number of revolutions, or complete four-stroke cycles, per minute. These two figures are always given with the engine data along with the horsepower.

Example: *Porsche 904 GTS*. Displacement 119.9 cu. in. (1,966 cc). Maximum horsepower 180 hp. (DIN) at 7,000 rpm. Maximum torque 147.6 fp. (DIN) at 5,000 rpm. Rated horsepower 91.6 hp. (DIN).

When the body of the car is removed, the engine and other interior parts are visible.

Example: *Ford Taunus 20 M*. Displacement 121.9 cu. in. (1,998 cc). Maximum horsepower 85 hp. (DIN) at 5,000 rpm. Maximum torque 108.7 fp. (DIN) at 3,000 rpm. Rated horsepower 42.5 hp. (DIN).

ANATOMY OF THE ENGINE

THE CARBURETOR

The carburetor mixes gasoline with air and sends some of the mixture to the cylinders, depending on how much power is required at that moment. The amount of gasoline/air mixture which is sent is controlled by the driver's foot on the accelerator. The gasoline pump, which can be electrical or mechanical, is what draws the gasoline from the tank to the carburetor. About 24 quarts (or liters) of air are mixed with a cubic centimeter of gasoline in the carburetor to make the proper mixture. Sometimes a greater proportion of gasoline is needed—for example when you start up or accelerate quickly.

The carburetor is a barrel or cup which always has a constant amount of gas in it, the level being maintained by a stopper, called a float. When the level goes down, the float does too, and the opening for filling the cup allows more gasoline in. As the level and float rise, the opening closes. In the bottom of the cup are two ducts, regulated by some screws with calibrated perforations, that link up with the carburetion chamber.

The carburetion chamber is a cylinder with an air filter at one end and the intake manifold—an opening—at the other. Near the center, the cylinder narrows so the air passing through it travels faster and with greater pressure. At the narrowest point is an opening that connects with the carburetor. Air passing through this narrow section sucks in a certain amount of liquid gasoline which is turned into a gas by mixing with the air. By pressing on the accelerator, the driver lets more gasoline enter through another duct. The carburetor divides into as many pipes as there are cylinders and connects with the inside of the cylinders by means of the intake valve in the cylinder.

Carburetors can be single barrel, with one carburetor for all the cylinders (this is normally used in passenger vehicles), or double, triple, or even quadruple barrel, where each barrel serves only some cylinders of the engine—normally only in high performance engines.

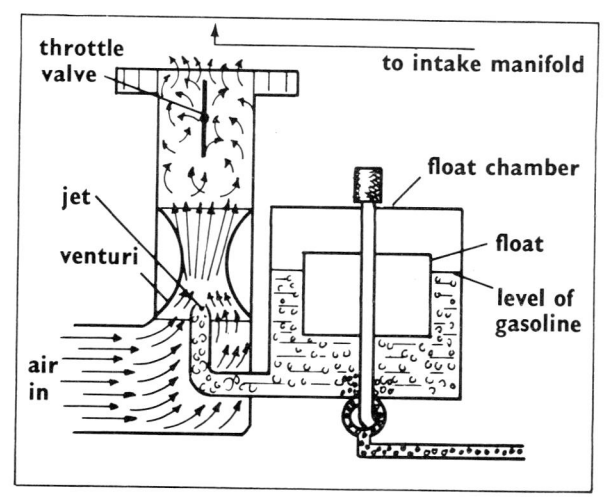

Simplified diagram of a carburetor.

FUEL INJECTION

Even though a fuel-injected engine is an expensive and delicate system, racing and high performance cars frequently use injector pumps. The pump controls the flow of gasoline perfectly at every moment, so it produces a consistently higher compression ratio than is possible with just a carburetor. (The compression ratio is the ratio between the volume of the cylinder with the piston at the top when combustion takes place, and with the piston at the bottom.)

Fuel injection can be direct or indirect. In direct fuel injection, the gasoline is injected right into the cylinder. In the indirect method, the gasoline goes to the intake manifold, still outside the intake valve. Direct fuel injectors are more expensive.

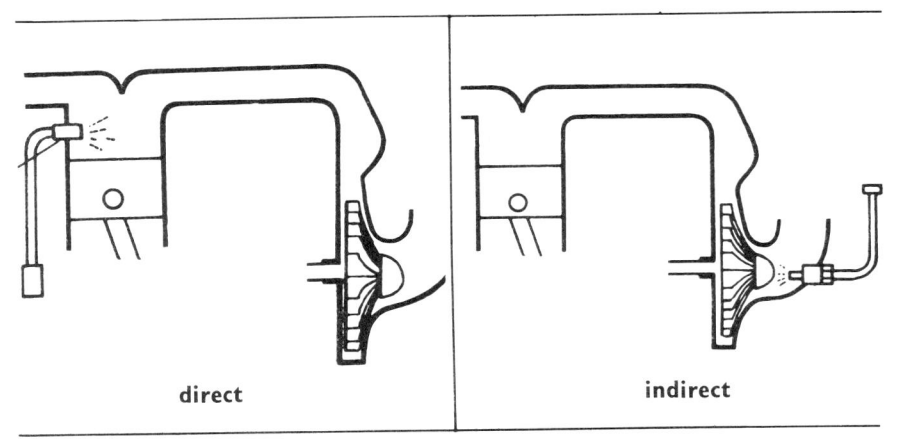

| direct | indirect |

With direct fuel injection, the injector pump delivers gasoline to the cylinder. With the indirect method, the gasoline goes to the intake manifold.

SUPERCHARGERS

In normal carburetion, the air mixed with the gasoline is at atmospheric pressure. Sports and competition cars are sometimes "souped up" by a supercharger, which shoots air into the carburetor under pressure. While this does provide more power, a supercharger requires a very strong engine. Because of the wear on the engine and the large amount of fuel used, superchargers are used on only a few competition cars.

The two most common types of superchargers are the centrifugal, which uses a kind of bladed wheel that forces the air into the carburetor; and the "Roots," made up of two parts which look like the halves of a figure eight. These two parts turn in opposite directions so that when one is vertical, the other is horizontal. This type of compressor is usually placed between the carburetor and the intake valve.

The supercharger can be powered by the engine itself, by a belt or gears, or by a turbine placed in the exhaust manifold and moved by the exhaust gases.

THE VALVES

In four-stroke engines the gas enters and exits the cylinders through valves. Valves can be either side valves or overhead valves, depending on their location. With overhead valves, the inside of the valve is above the piston, while side valves—rarely used nowadays—are at the side.

A perfectly running engine requires both the intake and exhaust valves to open and close at the right moment. This is the job of the camshaft. The operation is as follows: the crankshaft, which lies parallel to and below the camshaft, transmits movement to the camshaft (or shafts) with a chain called the timing chain (in passenger cars) or by a series of gears (in high performance cars). The camshaft is a piece of thick wire bent into a sort of staircase. At a certain point in the revolution of the camshaft, the high parts lift the corresponding valves, allowing gasoline and air to enter through the valve. When the valve is not lifted open by the camshaft, a strong spring holds it closed.

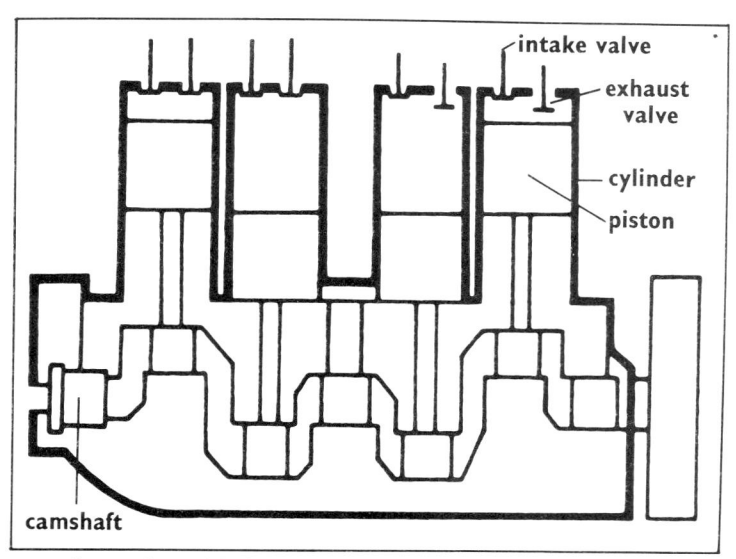

A four-stroke engine with four cylinders in a line. The camshaft raises and lowers the pistons in the cylinders.

IGNITION

The gasoline and air mixture in the cylinder is compressed when the piston moves up. When the piston compresses the mixture to a certain point, it is ignited by a spark from the spark plug.

The usual source of the spark is a battery that supplies a continuous low current (6 or 12 volts) that is transformed to a higher current by an electric coil with two windings, called the primary and secondary windings. Three conductor cables lead out from the electric coil; one from the secondary and two from the primary.

The cable from the secondary winding goes to the distributor, which directs the current to the spark plugs in the proper order. One of the primary cables goes to the contact, and the other goes to the condenser. When the primary winding is energized—"turned on"—this sets up a magnetic flux which, when broken, produces an electric current of several thousand volts in the secondary. This electricity goes to a spark plug through the points and the distributor. The high voltage here makes the spark jump the gap at the spark plug. The current which is drawn from the battery is replaced by the generator or (on modern cars) an alternator which is most effective at low speed.

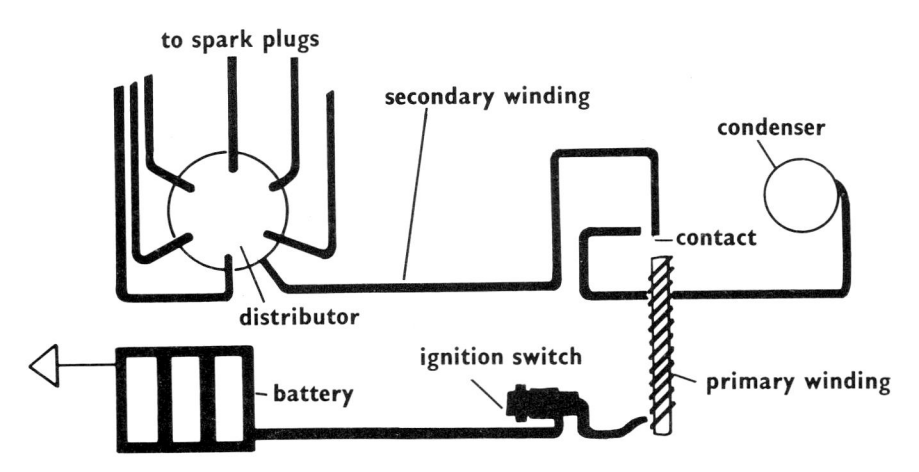

When the key turns in the ignition of a car, the battery is momentarily overloaded. This sets up a current of about 20,000 volts that ignites the spark plugs, starting the car. As the engine runs, the spark plugs ignite the gaseous mixture in the cylinders.

LUBRICATION

The pistons do not come directly in contact with the walls of the cylinder. Instead, rings—called piston rings—of harder material are lodged in grooves in the piston. The piston rings are broken by a cut, generally beveled, to make it easier to put them around the piston. Each piston usually has three rings at the top to keep the gas from escaping, and one at the bottom for lubrication. So that none of the compressed gases escape, the cut of each ring is in a different point around the piston.

In the two-stroke engine, a portion of oil is mixed with the gasoline to lubricate the piston. In the four-stroke engine, lubrication is different, however. Oil is kept in the pan at the bottom of the engine. A pump in the oil pan (called, of course, the oil pump) forces oil from the pan through a filter, then through special channels to all the points of the engine which need lubricating—the bearings of the crankshaft and camshaft, and then along the outside of the pistons, to distribute an oil film on the cylinder walls. Then the oil is scraped off the walls and falls back into the oil pan. This system provides a fine film of oil on all the moving parts.

Sports cars and competition engines use the dry pan system. In this case, the oil is in a container, and a pump circulates oil from the container to the engine. The high number of rpm's in competition engines makes the oil very hot, causing it to lose its lubricating qualities, so a small radiator to cool the oil is included in this system.

Racing cars have a gauge to indicate the exact pressure of the oil, which is usually measured in pounds per square inch. In family cars, however, the pressure gauge is replaced by a light that goes on if the pressure drops too low. This light needs only a single contact—much simpler than a gauge that indicates the exact pressure at every moment.

Various types of motor oil are available, differing mainly in their viscosity, or the way they stick to the engine's parts. Oil must be changed every season because it becomes more fluid and loses viscosity as the weather grows warmer. In summer or in hot climates a denser oil is necessary than in winter or in cold places. There are some multi-grade oils that can be used in a wide range of temperatures. Viscosity is measured in SAE units. SAE 20 oil flows more easily than SAE 40 oil.

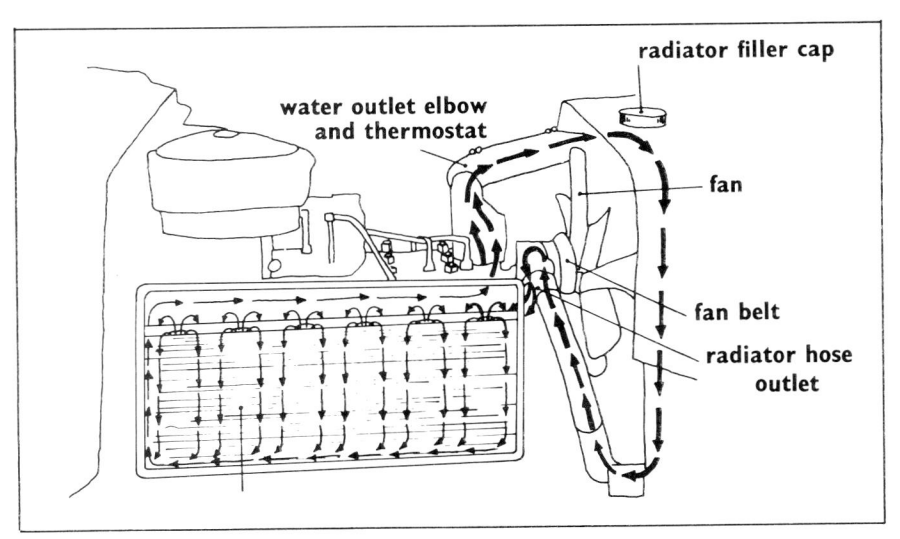

Water circulates in the radiator to cool the engine.

When the oil has been used for a while, it becomes filled with impurities and loses its viscous qualities. So it is necessary to change not only the filter, but also the oil itself, using a different grade of oil if necessary.

THE COOLING SYSTEM

The constant explosions of gasoline and air in the cylinders make a lot of heat, and this has to be reduced so the engine is not seriously damaged. The cooling system, which can be either air or liquid, takes care of this.

An air-cooled engine is very simple: the outside walls of the cylinders are exposed to the air flow produced by the car's own motion, or by a ventilating fan run by the engine itself. If there is no fan, the cooling system is at its simplest, but it depends entirely on the flow of air generated by the car's speed. Thus, when the car is idle or moving slowly—in city traffic or congested areas, for example—this type of cooling is not enough. The cool air is not forced through vents or the series of air ducts that lead to the cylinders. To increase the cooling, the outside walls of the cylinders often have fin-like projections that allow more air to flow through. This system of cooling is used in economy cars as well as competition cars (all Porsches, for example).

The liquid cooling system, whether the liquid is plain water or a mixture of water and other liquids to prevent freezing (antifreeze) passes between the cylinder walls, the radiator, the cylinder head and block. The radiator is a series of narrow pipes surrounded by a mesh of thin metal, which forms a wide surface for contact with the air. Air is forced through the radiator by a ventilator fan activated by the engine itself.

Circulation between the cold water in the radiator and the hot water from the engine is carried out by what is called the thermosyphon effect, where hot water rises. Here, the hot water rises and passes through the radiator to be cooled, while the cold water is forced down to the engine. This system has been improved by using a water pump, mounted on the same shaft used for the ventilator fan, to force the water to circulate in the engine block. Since the motor requires a certain temperature for best performance, a thermostat is included in the cooling system. The thermostat halts the flow of water to the radiator until a certain temperature is reached (about 158° F); then a valve in the thermostat opens to let the liquid circulate again.

THE CLUTCH

The clutch is located between and connects the engine and the transmission. When it is stepped on, the circular plates the clutch is made of separate from each other, allowing the engine to run free of the transmission. The clutch transfers the engine's power to the drive wheels smoothly and gradually.

In cars without automatic transmission, the most commonly used clutch is the disc type. This basically consists of two plates,

When the clutch pedal is depressed, the gears can be shifted to get more or less power from the engine.

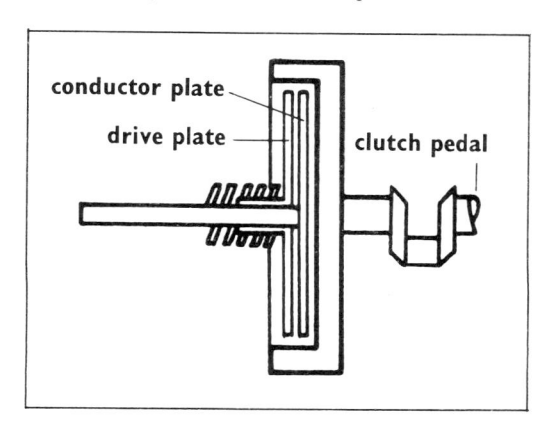

conductor plate
drive plate
clutch pedal

47

the conductor or pressure plate, and the conducted or drive plate. These plates are in tight contact with each other while the car is in neutral. When the clutch pedal is depressed, the pressure plate separates from the drive plate and the gears can be shifted.

The contact surface of these plates is non-metallic. They are wrapped with pressed layers of asbestos and reinforced with copper filaments, for a good contact surface that resists heat and wear.

Other types of clutches are multiple discs, bell action, centrifugal, semi-centrifugal, and hydraulic.

TRANSMISSION, STEERING AND BRAKES

THE TRANSMISSION

The transmission allows the engine and the drive wheels to turn at a convenient speed, according to the resistance (hills, bumpy roads, or starting up) that the engine must overcome.

The transmission consists of two shafts: the primary, which is a continuation of the clutch shaft, and the secondary; these shafts are parallel to each other. Each shaft has a series of pinions or gears that can mesh together in several combinations. All the transmission's parts are enclosed in metal, in an oil bath that constantly lubricates the gears.

When the car is in neutral, none of the pinions of the two shafts are engaged or locked together. The car can stand still while the engine is on, without your foot on the clutch pedal.

When you shift to first gear, a small pinion of the primary shaft engages with a larger pinion of the secondary shaft. The engine runs slowly now, but powerfully—necessary when starting up or climbing a steep hill. A typical ratio of the two gears is 10 sprockets of the primary shaft gear engaged with 30 sprockets of the secondary shaft gear (10/30).

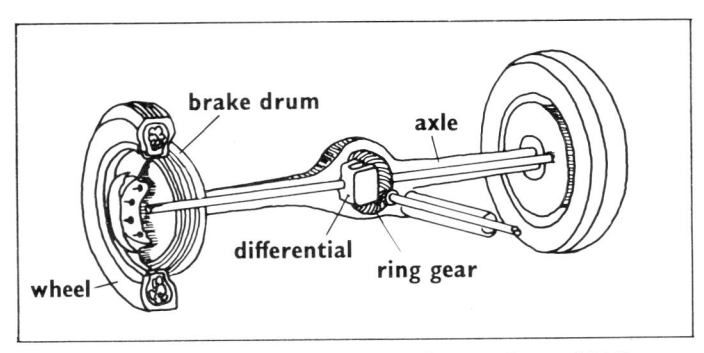

The differential prevents the car from skidding every time you turn a corner by allowing the rear wheels to spin independently of each other.

In second gear, the next-size pinion of the primary shaft (15 sprockets) engages with a pinion of 25 sprockets of the secondary shaft. The car can go a little faster and is just a bit more powerful.

For high, or third gear, two pinions of an equal number of sprockets are meshed, for a 1/1 ratio between the two pinions. The speed of the car is then equal to the output of the engine.

When a larger pinion of the primary shaft is engaged with a smaller pinion of the secondary shaft, for example 22/18, you have overdrive, or fourth gear. The car can go very quickly with little effort by the engine.

You often need reverse gear to manoeuvre a car. A certain gear that changes the revolutions of the engine to the opposite direction is used, and the car can back up. Reverse speed is similar to first speed, since the car needs a great effort from the engine to move.

This is only a simplified form of the function of the transmission. In competition cars there are more forward speeds, and in some automatic transmission is used for the driver's comfort. This deprives the driver of full participation, however, and is considered unsporting.

THE DIFFERENTIAL

To understand what the differential does, imagine a parade in which the formation of soldiers must turn to the right. To keep all the soldiers in a straight line, those at the right must slow down while those at the left speed up.

A car works the same way when it turns a corner or goes around a curve. Each wheel must travel a different distance, and so has to turn at a different speed. There is no problem with the front wheels if the car has rear-wheel drive, since they are not connected to the same axle: each front wheel turns independently of the other. The rear wheels—in this case the traction wheels—must turn at different speeds, however, while they are connected to the same axle. This is the job of the differential.

Located in the middle of the rear axle, the differential consists of a pinion gear at the end of the transmission shaft that joins with the ring gear. The ring gear, a gear which stands on its edge, is connected to a series of gears—satellite and planetary gears—that attach to each half of the rear axle. As the halves of the axle work independently of each other, so do the rear wheels they connect to. All these mechanisms are enclosed in a housing immersed in a bath of high density oil.

THE BRAKES

When the car is in motion, you can reduce its speed by simply lifting your foot off the accelerator. Once the accelerator is not operated, the engine reduces the number of revolutions per minute, and the car travels more slowly. This is called the motor brake, and it is even more effective if you shift to a lower gear too.

Of course, all cars have a braking system which operates independently of the engine. Imagine a car that rolls down a smooth grade with its engine stopped. Because of the car's weight, the speed increases more and more. To stop the car, there must be a resisting force on the turning wheels. This is the principle of the brake, and it is as old as the horse-drawn carriage.

The drum brake consists of a drum—a hollow cylinder—which is connected to the wheel and turns with it. When the brake pedal inside the car is pressed, it compresses the liquid inside the master cylinder, which in turn forces liquid in the wheel cylinder to move the brake shoes. The shoes press against the drums at each wheel, and the wheels stop turning. When the brake pedal is released, a spring makes the shoes close together, leaving the drum to turn freely again.

Since the drum is metallic, the shoes cannot be metallic too, since the friction of metal on metal would create a lot of heat and not be too effective. The outside surfaces of the shoes are lined

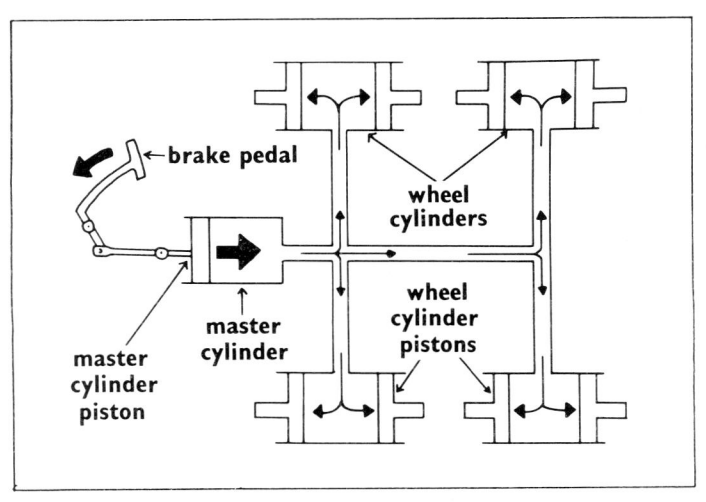

When you put your foot on the brake pedal, the pressure forces the brake shoes against the drum or disc, slowing the wheel down.

with an asbestos material that is resistant to fraying, even with much friction, and very resistant to heat.

Drum brakes have been replaced by disc brakes on most new cars. A disc brake consists of a metal disc, about 12″ in diameter and 6″ thick, that is joined to the wheel or the axle. The disc turns inside a pair of pincer-type grips, on the interior of which are shoes. When the brake pedal is stepped on, the grips press the shoes against the disc, producing a braking action. This is similar to the operation of a bicycle brake, where the shoes rub against the rim of the wheel, instead of against the faces of the disc.

The disc brake has several advantages over the classic drum brake: first, it can be cooled much better, since the disc is outside and has a large surface over which the heat can spread. Furthermore, it is much lighter in weight and has almost no distortion, or uneven braking on the wheels. Since the brakes in competition cars are constantly used, disc brakes are preferred to drum brakes since drum brakes wear out faster.

Power brakes are often installed now. These save effort for the driver and have a double hydraulic circuit for greater security. Compressed air brakes and electric brakes are normally used only in heavy transport vehicles.

STEERING

To change the direction that the car travels, you turn the steering wheel. The size of the steering wheel varies according to the type of vehicle it steers: it is very large in trucks, and very small in single-seat racing cars. The steering wheel extends through a shaft in the steering column to a gearbox, that contains the gears that transform the movement of the steering wheel into a movement of the front wheels.

The amount that the steering wheel turns is not the same amount that the front wheels turn, since there are pinions and gears that change the rotary motion of the steering wheel into horizontal motion at the wheels and magnify the turn that you make. In trucks and heavy vehicles, the ratio between the amount the wheels turn and the amount the driver turns the steering wheel is very large. In competition cars, where curves are taken quickly and precisely, the ratio is much smaller, until the tiny kart, where the steering is direct—that is, every inch the steering wheel is turned moves the wheels the same amount. In heavy vehicles and some passenger cars, power steering reduces driving effort considerably.

There are two main types of steering gear: first, the "endless screw," called worm and sector, in which a screw thread in the steering column operates a toothed section that transmits the movement along a tie rod to the front wheels; and second, the "ratchet" system, in which a pinion operates a horizontal toothed bar called a ratchet, whose lateral movement is transmitted to the wheels.

CHASSIS AND BODY

THE CHASSIS

This is a vital part of the car, since it is the frame upon which rest all the other elements of the car. Chassis have changed through the years, and they were at one time even eliminated. In some cars the body, not the chassis, is the rigid element which supports all the other elements. While this type of body has a series of reinforcement components, it is not really a chassis.

Since the first automobiles were really horse-drawn carriages with an engine instead of a horse, the chassis and body were the same as those used in the carriages. The oldest type of chassis, used for many years, was simply a derivation of those and consisted of two main elements: a pair of parallel bars joined by other bars lying across them, like a ladder. Later, the bars were replaced by bars in an X. A tubular chassis, used in high perform-

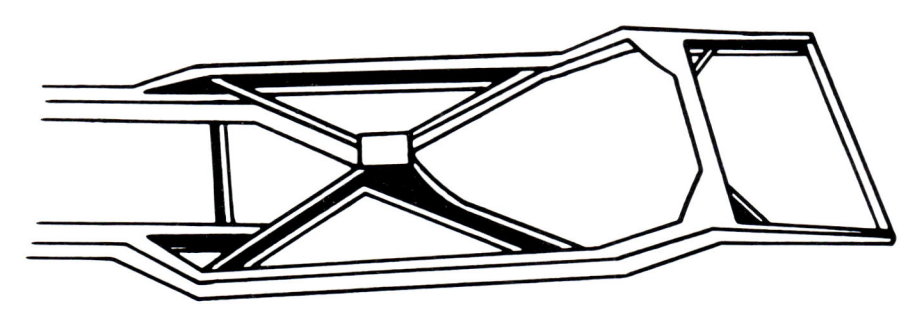

A chassis with the bars placed in an X is used in passenger vehicles.

tubular chassis

monocoque chassis

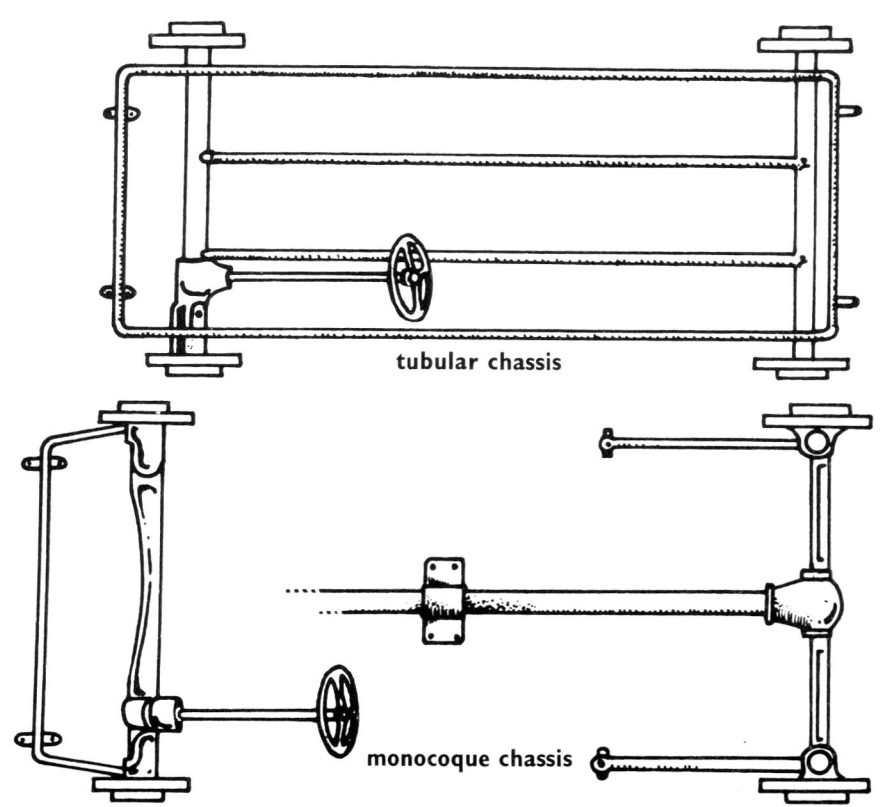

Metal tubes rather than flat bars make up the tubular chassis (above). The monocoque chassis is a light but rigid shell forming the outline of the car.

ance cars, has tubular metal parts, rather than flat bars. The multi-tubular chassis uses lighter elements and so is less heavy yet more rigid than other types of chassis. These conditions are very important in competition driving, where complicated multi-tubular chassis (those used by some Maseratis, for example) have the name of "Birdcage" because of their intricate structure.

The aeronautic technique of a single shell or monocoque structure has been used, mainly in formula cars. Given an equal rigidity, the monocoque chassis is lighter and more resistant than the multi-tubular, and it offers greater protection to the driver. It is, however, more expensive to build and harder to repair. For these reasons, the monocoque structure is generally used only in single-seat racing cars.

THE BODY

The body is the most visible and distinguishing factor of a car. In designing a car body, aesthetic factors as well as aerodynamics come into play, especially in competition cars, since the stability of the car depends on the shape of the car body. The way the air currents hit the car makes one type of body more sensible than another in a cross wind. So the design of the body is also crucial to the car's performance.

For many years it was thought that very streamlined shapes were best for competition cars. But then someone realized something that has turned out to be very valuable for stability: instead of a thin tapered tail with a sharp point, a new type of tail was used that creates a pocket of air under itself, increasing the traction of the rear end.

Another thing that increased the grip of the rear wheels was an

Long, low and lean, a racing car's streamlined body is designed for the least wind resistance.

aileron, like a control flap on an airplane, at the end of the car's body. Ailerons are used on almost all Formula 1 cars.

The bodies were originally made of wood, but later sheet metal was used. Now modern plastic products are preferred because of their strength and durability.

According to the different types of bodies, cars are classified this way:

SEDAN. Closed body with four or six seats in two rows, and two or four doors.

LIMOUSINE. Body with four doors and two rows of fixed seats, plus one row of folding seats, for from six to nine seats.

CONVERTIBLE. Car with a folding canvas top and glass windows.

ROADSTER. Like the convertible, but more of a sports car. In Italy it is called a "spider."

COUPE. A two-door car, usually having only two seats, or with another two very small seats in the back.

STATION WAGON. A very versatile car, thanks to the fifth door in back that lowers. Luggage or packages can be stored behind the seats. It contains up to nine seats.

SEDAN DE VILLE or LANDAULET. Typical car of millionaires or celebrities, with a separation between the driver and the rear seats and a sliding or folding roof in the driver's compartment.

SUSPENSION

When a car moves along a road—even a road in perfect condition—there are always small bumps and holes to travel over. If it were not for the suspension, not only would the ride be very bumpy, but the car's stability would also be gravely endangered. The elements that absorb these small bumps are the tires, several types of springs, and the shock absorbers.

The tires are the first things to touch the ground. They can absorb up to about 1½" of unevenness before the other elements are needed.

One kind of spring is the laminated leaf spring, which is a carry-over from the horse-drawn carriage. This spring is a series of semi-elliptical steel leaves of graduated sizes. The ends of the biggest leaf are attached to the chassis, while the rear axle is inserted in the center of the spring. When the car goes over a bump, the leaf spring flattens and absorbs a great part of the bounce.

Another type of spring is the torsion bar. This is a steel bar

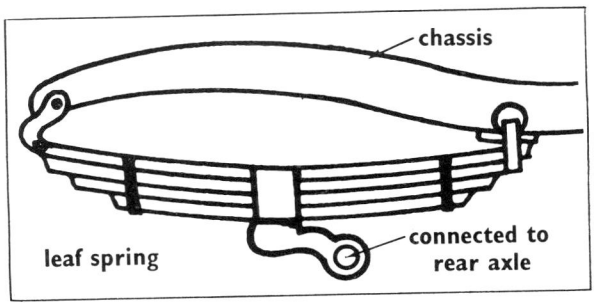

The largest leaf of a leaf spring is connected to the chassis, and the smallest leaf to the rear axle.

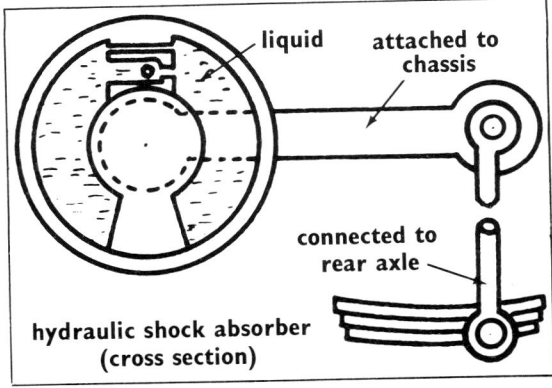

When the wheels (located behind the liquid in the illustration) hit a bump, the liquid in the shock absorbers is compressed, and the chassis does not bounce.

attached at one end to the chassis, and at the other end to the rear axle by means of a short lever arm. The bar twists when the tire and the axle meet a bump, and recovers its shape when the bump disappears.

The shock absorbers control the springs' tendency to bounce and prevent the springs' compressing and expanding unnecessarily. They may be the friction type, or, more commonly, the hydraulic type. In hydraulic shock absorbers, a cylinder fitted with a piston and plunger rod is filled with a liquid. One end is attached to the chassis and the other to the axle. When the car hits a bump, the liquid slowly absorbs the shock.

Because of the car's suspension, the body and therefore the driver do not bounce with every bump on the road. If the tires do not absorb the bumps, the springs or shock absorbers should.

THE MOST FAMOUS CARS

Since the automobile was invented nearly a century ago, there have been dozens of cars that have come and gone. The more successful ones—that is, those that have won races—are still being manufactured. When other cars beat them too often, they too will fade from the racing scene, as manufacturers challenge each other to design the perfect racing car.

Here is a brief summary of some of the most famous racing cars, with three recent makes described in more detail:

BRABHAM

Driver Jack Brabham and designer Ron Tauranac joined in 1961 to form Motor Racing Developments, of Byfleet, England. The first car, a Formula Junior, was called the MRD, but since then the cars have been known as Brabhams. In 1966, Jack Brabham made history by becoming the first World Champion to win this title while driving a car of his own make. In 1967, Denny Hulme won the championship in a Brabham, and the car is still successful today.

BRM

Former racing driver Raymond Mays's original idea was to have financial and technical backing from all the British motor and accessory firms, to build a superior British car. Not all the

An uphill climb on the circuit at Brands Hatch, in England.

Scenes like this close call are not infrequent. Drivers must have fast reflexes to avoid serious accidents.

companies went along with this, however, so the first car was not raced until 1950, a year behind schedule. The car was a very advanced machine, and finally won a World Championship race in 1959, the Dutch Grand Prix. In 1962, Graham Hill drove a BRM V-8 and won the World Championship. The BRM, with some changes, is still a racing success.

CHAPARRAL

An American car, the Chaparral is a unique racing car, as it has automatic transmission and does not hesitate to use unusual advanced techniques. The first car was built in 1961 and was quite successful until 1968. In 1966, large aerofoils, or wings, were added above the rear wheels, creating quite a commotion in racing circles. New regulations in 1969 restricted these attachments, and the 1969 CanAm Chaparral, the 2H, was a failure.

COOPER

Manufacturing motorcycle engines at first, the Coopers—father Charles and son John—switched to Formula 2 cars in 1957. A rear 2,000 cc engine, which allowed the Coopers to race in Formula 1 competition, helped Stirling Moss win the 1958 Argentine Grand Prix. Driving for Cooper, Jack Brabham won the World Championship in both 1959 and 1960, but in the next decade, as other cars raced rear-engine machines, Coopers lost their superiority. In 1968, Cooper withdrew from the racing scene and all the equipment was sold.

Cars in a pack round a corner in the Italian Grand Prix at Monza.

EAGLE

Another driver to build his own racing car was American Dan Gurney. The designers of the chassis and the engine were both British, but the car was manufactured in California. The most successful race for the Eagle was a win in the 1967 Belgian Grand Prix. The Eagle has also performed well at Indianapolis three years in a row: Gurney placed second in 1968 behind another Eagle, second in 1969, and third in 1970.

ERA

Successful in the 1930's, the ERA can be considered a forerunner of the BRM, as its designers went to BRM after World War II. The most successful ERA was a single-seater with a 6-cylinder, 1,500 cc supercharged engine.

FERRARI

There is a small factory in Modena, Italy that was founded by Enzo Ferrari, an outstanding car driver. The factory produces not only prestige sports cars, but also single-seaters and prototypes.

After World War II, Ferrari began its construction of sports cars with the 125, with a 12 engine. This car was the first of a large number of successes. In 1949 the Le Mans 24 Hours was won by a Ferrari 166 MM, driven by Luigi Chenetti and Selsdon. In 1951, a 350 "Mexico" won the hard Pan-American race, where another Ferrari took second place. Following this, the 250 MM won the 1,000 Miles; the 340 MM was victor in the 1,000 Miles of 1953; and the 375 Plus, which in 1954 also returned with Trintignant and Gonzalez to win the Le Mans 24 Hours. With the 290 MM, Ferrari took the first five places in the 1,000 Miles of 1956. In 1958 the 250 TR (Testa Rosa) appeared, and then there was a new Ferrari triumph at Le Mans with Phil Hill and Gendebien. This initiated an uninterrupted series of successes at Le Mans until 1966, when it was beaten by its rival, Ford.

The 330 TR/LM was the last Ferrari with an engine in the front that was already taking on aspects of the new prototypes.

The 250 P, the first Ferrari prototype with a central engine, won at the Sebring 12 Hours, at Nürburgring, and at Le Mans, placing there in the first four places.

In 1964 the 330 P appeared. That year, the "Caballino Rampante" won at Sebring, Nürburgring, Le Mans (in the first

After being unloaded from the transport truck at the track, the competition car must undergo a thorough examination.

65

three places), the Reims 12 Hours, the 1,000 Kilometers of Paris, and the Tourist Trophy. The 330 P-2 came out in 1965, and triumphed in the tortuous circuit of Nürburgring. The last Ferrari triumph in Le Mans was obtained thanks to a 275 LM. Very different from the previous prototype models is the 330 P-3 of 1966, with 420 hp., but this cannot beat its rival Ford which managed to win the three first places in Le Mans, as well as other victories with its MK II. The last of the Ferrari prototypes is the P-4, outwardly similar to the P-3, but with a different engine: it has 450 hp. and a maximum speed of 198 mph. This car won at Daytona and Monza, but the MK Ford won the Le Mans 24 Hours in 1967, while Ferrari took the second and third places.

Ferrari prepared another car in 1967 for the Canadian American Challenge Cup (CanAm)—its 350 CanAm, a two-seat racer of 254.7 cu. in. (4,176 cc). Only the 365 P-2 of 1965 surpassed it in cylinder capacity (it had a 267.8 cu. in. [4,390 cc] engine). The car could not beat its American rivals, however. In 1968, Ferrari retired from prototype races by showing the super-stylized P-5 without having raced it.

FORD

The name Ford is an old one in car manufacturing, but the Ford prototype racing car is very new. When the old Henry Ford began manufacturing cars, he realized that races were an excellent means of publicity. His monstrous 999, with its 1,019 cu. in. (16,708 cc) engine, gained attention in 1903. Many years later, Henry Ford III came to the same conclusion about racing and tried to buy out Ferrari. Negotiations fell through, however, so Ford started to make his own prototype, derived from the experimental Mustang I. This apparently was the true starting point for the Ford GT-40 MK I. This was furnished with a 256 cu. in. (4,200 cc) V-8 engine in a central position, producing 350 hp. It appeared unsuccessfully in the 1964 season. It was modified in 1965: the front end was totally redesigned and the wheel radius was changed. A 288.3 cu. in. (4,727 cc) engine gave the GT-40 its first success at Daytona, with an average speed of 99.9 mph.

A new model, the MK II, with a 427 cu. in. (7,000 cc) engine and 475 h.p., achieved its first success in the 1966 Daytona race, and also gave Ford its first victory at Le Mans.

Ford did not rest there: he prepared a new, totally different prototype in which the most modern techniques of aerodynamic construction were employed. This Ford J did not race in the first trials in April, 1967, but was modified in August. It was tested at Riverside with an accident that killed Ken Miles.

The Ford J was abandoned, but it was developed into the modern MK IV that was a resounding success at Le Mans in 1967, giving Ford the second victory in this circuit. The life of this promising prototype was over with the 1968 regulation which limited the prototype displacement to 183 cu. in. (3,000 cc), and that of the sports car to 305 cu. in. (5,000 cc). This let Ford use his GT-40 as a sports car; this was manufactured on a small scale and won several races, among them the third consecutive win at Le Mans. It is too bad that the regulation regarding cylinder capacity cut short the successful record of the MK IV.

JAGUAR

Designed by Sir William Lyons, Jaguar racing cars were most successful in the early 1950's, when the XK120C (known as the C-type) won the Le Mans 24 Hours in both 1951 and 1953.

Well-known as a manufacturer of passenger cars, Ford also makes outstanding competition cars.

A new model on the track never fails to arouse the curiosity of onlookers.

The car is taken apart for a final check before the race.

Another version, the D-type, won at Le Mans in 1955, 1956 and 1957. No Jaguar cars have raced since then, although the road cars are still popular today.

LOTUS

In 1948, builder Colin Chapman developed a 1930 Austin 7 sedan into a trial car he named Lotus. Chapman gradually turned

Waiting to be worked on, a car rests in its transportation box.

his company, Lotus Engineering, into the largest racing car manufacturer in the world. Based in England, Lotus builds cars for almost every racing car formula, as well as road cars.

MARCH

Quite new in racing, March Engineering has been successful in Formula 1, Formula 2, Formula 3, Formula Ford and CanAm racing. Four Englishmen formed the company, which was unknown until 1970. Jackie Stewart won the 1970 Spanish Grand Prix in a March-Ford—a good beginning for an exciting new car.

McLAREN

Bruce McLaren was a member of the Cooper racing team until 1965, but in that year he began building his own racing cars. They were extremely successful—McLarens won the 1967, 1968 and 1969 CanAm championships. McLaren himself was killed in June, 1970 while testing a CanAm car, but the factory in England is still producing cars.

Coming round a curve is a Porsche, which has lately been one of the most successful racing cars.

The Porsche won the coveted World Sports Car Manufacturers' Championship in both 1969 and 1970.

MERCEDES-BENZ

Probably the oldest car manufacturing company still in business, Mercedes-Benz was begun by Gottlieb Daimler and Carl Benz. The Mercedes-Benz racing cars were most successful just before World War II, with some further success in the 1950's, but since then these cars have stayed out of racing.

PORSCHE

Ferdinand Porsche was born in 1875, and by 1900 had already built his first racing car with an electric engine. He dedicated his entire life to constructing automobiles—among them, the famous Volkswagen—but he did not found his own factory until 1950, when he used his name as the name of the car (although the first Porsche prototype was built in Austria in 1948). Porsche's factory was mainly dedicated to building sports cars from 40 to 44 hp. These models—the 356—were practically without change until 1959, when the new 911 (now, the 912) appeared. All the cars were faithful to the original specifications of Dr. Porsche: they had a rear air-cooled engine with four or more horizontal and opposite cylinders. During the 1950's, Porsches took part in numerous competitions—Liége-Rome-Liége, Pan-American, Le Mans and many others.

After Dr. Porsche's death in 1959, his son Ferry continued building cars, still according to his father's formula. Formula 1 and 2 single-seaters were also built between 1959 and 1962.

In 1963 a new competition Porsche was presented, the beginning of a new competitive line. This was the 904 GTS whose body was made of very light plastic. The engine had four cylinders, with 119.9 cu. in. (1,966 cc) and 180 hp. (DIN), for a maximum speed of 160 mph. The car triumphed right down the line: in the 1964 Targa Florio, where it won the two first

The car with the best time in the trials is given the best position in the starting line-up of the race.

After some minor damage is repaired, the car leaves the pits to rejoin the race.

places; in Nürburgring, where it placed third, fifth, sixth, and from eighth to twelfth place.

In 1965, a GTS placed fifth in the Daytona 24 Hours, behind the powerful Ford and Cobra. At Sebring, it took fifth and sixth places, and in Targa Florio, a Spyder took second, and a 904 placed third, fourth and fifth. At Le Mans, a six-cylinder 904 won fourth place.

In 1966 the Carrera-6 appeared, which, with its 122 cu. in. (2,000 cc) cylinder capacity, placed fourth at Sebring, behind

A Porsche glistens in the sun at Le Mans.

73

two 7,000 cc and one 5,000 cc Ford. The Carrera-6 was fourth and fifth at Monza, the winner at Targa Florio, fourth at Nürburgring, and from fourth to seventh at Le Mans.

In 1967, with the Carrera-6 modified into a sports model, the Carrera-10 prototype made its debut at Sebring. It won third and fourth places there, third at Monza, second at Spa-Francorchamps, and the first three places at Targa Florio. After winning the first four places at Nürburgring, a new 907 took fifth at Le Mans, immediately followed by a 910 (Carrera-10) and by two Carrera-6's. The car repeated the success of Targa Florio at Mugello, where it won the first three places.

From this point on, the Porsche's story was successful almost everywhere it raced—at Sebring in 1968, Targa Florio in the same year, Monte Carlo in 1970. The first Porsche win at Le Mans was in 1970, when Dickie Attwood and Hans Herrmann drove a Porsche 917 to first place. The crowning glory for Porsche was its being awarded the World Sports Car Manufacturers' Championship in both 1969 and 1970.

Such awards inspire car manufacturers to develop the best possible automobiles, while drivers are encouraged, through competition, to improve their driving and speed records. With cars and drivers always striving to outdo each other, auto racing will remain an exciting sport.

Mechanics adjust the wheels on Jackie Stewart's car before the trials for the Spanish Grand Prix.

SPORTS TRIALS

RALLIES

Rallies are the most available trials for anyone interested in automotive sports. You can use normal, everyday cars, but to make a good showing, it is wise to prepare the car.

The competition takes place on public roads, according to a route which has been marked out by the organization sponsoring the rally. Part of the run consists of complementary trials that might judge regularity and speed, on stretches closed to normal highway traffic. In the regularity trials, the object is to stay within a given time limit so that the car passes certain points along the route at an exact time. There are penalties for reaching the points too soon, as well as too late. In the speed trials, also known as chronometric runs, the object is to spend the least possible time in making a designated run.

Because cars of various classes and categories participate in the rallies, and because there are many trials within each class, the winners are determined by applying certain formulas. Normally, two types of winners are established: an overall winner, called "scratch," and others according to the individual classes of cars.

In a rally, each car has two crew members, the driver and the co-pilot or navigator, whose job is to make a precise chart of the

Coming around a curve.

route and use chronometers to mark off times. Both members of the crew must have the appropriate licenses to take part.

In this type of trial, the training is very important. This involves making a run before the competition itself, noticing the peculiarities of the route, and remembering where it is necessary to shift gears, brake, or accelerate. All this is meticulously recorded and "sung" during the run by the co-pilot, a big help for the driver.

As the cars approach the final turn, excitement peaks.

There are many classes of rallies—the famous one at Monte Carlo, which takes place over a long and difficult route with many stretches of ice and snow; the famous rally raced by professionals from Liége to Rome to Liége, of more than 2,400 miles; as well as other more modest rallies, organized by clubs on weekends, providing good ways to become active in auto racing.

HILL CLIMBS

These are contested on mountain highways which are closed to normal traffic. Their routes are difficult stretches to make the trial most interesting.

The cars start one by one at specified intervals according to an order set out by the sponsoring organization. The object is to make the run in the least amount of time. To do this, it is extremely important to know how to take advantage of the numerous curves, and to know the most appropriate times to change gears.

The starting times are precisely recorded, as are the finishing times, to figure how long each car takes. The classifications are usually also made by categories, as a "general" or a "scratch." In this popular type of trial, a wide range of cars is admitted, from the modest kart to the formula car, as well as a variety of touring cars, grand touring cars, sports cars, sports-prototypes and two-seat racers. This is the only type of trial where Group 7 competition cars are admitted in Europe.

There are many national and international championships organized for hill climbs. A certain number of races are run, each one worth a certain number of points depending on the difficulty of the race. The driver with the most points is champion. These races are often organized by clubs, and serve as a good starting point for auto racing. The appropriate license is required, as well as safety equipment: crash helmet, seat belt, fire extinguisher, and other items. The championship of Europe is one of the most important hill climbs. A series of trials is included in the championship—one of them, the climb to Montseny in Spain, is 10 miles long, a great distance if you are travelling over tortuous roads. For this event, car manufacturers as great as Porsche and Ferrari build special Group 7 cars.

Hill climbs are very popular, and not only among the

Curves on a race track call upon the skills of the drivers and fine-tuned engines, steering and transmissions in the cars. Because of the high speeds of the races, curves are usually "banked."

participants. They also attract many followers, some of whom travel far to watch a race. By arriving beforehand, they choose observation points where they can judge for themselves the capabilities of the drivers.

Good driving training is basic to hill climbing, to plan the curves wisely and to use the transmission, brakes, and accelerator in the best possible ways. The cars are sometimes specially prepared so they can put out more in a climb; these preparations are authorized only in certain competition cars, however.

The stands are filled as a car makes its way to the starting line.

SPEED RACES

Speed trials are usually carried out either in permanent circuits built just for this purpose, like the Jarama circuit in Madrid, or on highways which are closed to normal traffic during the trials, like the Targa Florio in Sicily. A circuit through city streets is sometimes plotted, but this never offers the same safety conditions to either the drivers or the spectators as permanent speed circuits do.

Cars are placed in several rows according to the times they raced in the trials. Usually the engines are going and the cars are

Drivers and navigators discuss their chances before the start of a big race. Flags in foreground stand ready to signal drivers.

81

stopped when the start is signalled with the national flag. Another type of start, the flying start, is frequently used in the United States: the cars follow the judge's car for one lap around the circuit, keeping in the starting formation. When they get near the starting line, the judge's car gets off the track and the participants accelerate. This system has the advantage of preventing collisions—sometimes cars stall at the start and block

A driver waves as the black and white checkered flag signals the finish of the race.

Drivers dash to their cars in the start known as "Le Mans."

the ones behind them. Some endurance trials use the start known as "Le Mans"; this is used in the famous Le Mans 24 Hours, the Sebring 12 Hours, and other races. For this start, the cars are placed in a diagonal to one side of the track according to their training times, and the drivers are on the other side of the track. When the signal is given, the drivers run across the track, get in their cars, start the engines and begin.

Some races are based on a certain number of laps around the circuit, often naming the race—Indianapolis's 500 Miles, or Nürburgring's 1,000 Km., for example. The winner is signalled with the black and white checkered flag. The order of the rest of the participants is based on the difference of minutes and seconds among those who completed the laps, and by the number of laps that those who did not finish are lacking. For example, the results of the 1968 European Grand Prix: 1st, J. Stewart, 2 hr. 19 min. 3.2 sec.; 2nd, G. Hill, by 4 min. 3.1 sec. . . . 11th, J. Oliver, by one lap.

Careful! It's easy to skid off the track in the rain. Besides inconveniencing the race, rain is dangerous to drive in.

Still other races are based on time, as in the Sebring 12 Hours, the Le Mans 24 Hours, etc. In these cases the winner is the driver who has travelled farthest in that time.

Car racing marshals stand around the entire circuit so they can signal the drivers with an international code of flags.

The NATIONAL FLAG signals the start and the BLACK AND WHITE CHECKERED FLAG, the finish.

BLUE held still: another driver is following closely.

BLUE being waved: another driver is going to pass.

WHITE: an ambulance or other service vehicle is on the track.

YELLOW held still: danger; passing is prohibited.

YELLOW being waved: grave danger; prepare for braking.

YELLOW WITH RED VERTICAL STRIPES: oil is spilled on the track.
GREEN: no longer any danger.
RED: immediate stop (this flag is only handled by the judge).
BLACK (with a number): the vehicle with such a number should leave the track immediately. Either a rule has been broken or the car is in a dangerous condition.

These are not the only signals that the drivers receive. The members of their team show on large blackboards their position in the race, the distance between them and the car ahead, the number of laps completed, that they should speed up or slow down, that they need a pit stop, etc.—all according to a code arranged before the race between the driver and the members of his team. These signals are usually made from the pits (the stalls set up for repairing each car). Sometimes the pits are too far away for the fast-moving driver to see the signals easily. Then the signals are placed in a more visible spot, like at the end of the sharp turn at Mulsanne, in Le Mans.

While the first two cars are several yards apart, the difference is slight at great speeds.

THE MOST FAMOUS RACES

The main competitions of single-seat racing cars—that is, Formula 1—form a series of trials, each worth a certain number of points. At the end of that year's racing, each driver's points are added, to decide who is the world champion driver. For example, the most important hill climbs combine to form the well-known Mountain Championship of Europe. There are many other types of trials which make up more series of championships—too many to list here.

WORLD CHAMPIONSHIP OF DRIVERS

The world driving championship is a title which has been contested unceasingly since 1950, when Nino Farina was declared champion with 30 points, beating Juan Manuel Fangio by only 3. Farina won the Grand Prix of Great Britain, Italy, and Switzerland, and Fangio won those of Belgium, France, and Monaco, both with an Alfa-Romeo.

In 1951, the determined Fangio became champion, with 31 points; Alberto Ascari was second, with 27. Fangio won the Grand Prix of Spain, France and Switzerland with an Alfa-Romeo. Ascari won those of Germany and Italy with a Ferrari.

A new name was added to the list of champions in 1952, when Alberto Ascari won a total of 36 points (versus 24 by Farina), winning in Germany, Belgium, France, Great Britain, and Italy. In 1953, Ascari was champion again, with Fangio as runner-up, winning the same number of trials as in the previous year.

For four years after 1954, the great Fangio kept the title of champion; Gonzalez placed second in 1954; and in the next three years, Stirling Moss was runner-up.

Mike Hawthorn became champion in 1958, with Moss as second again. Stirling Moss, incidentally, won more races than Hawthorn—but the points that Hawthorn acquired by finishing in other positions totaled more than Moss's. Moss won the Grands Prix of Argentina, Holland, Monaco and Portugal, while the champion won only the Grand Prix of France.

In 1959, the Australian Jack Brabham won the championship;

Three-time world champion Jack Brabham pushes his car off the track after a mechanical failure destroys his chances of winning the race.

87

Engines ready, drivers and cars in place for the start, and a few last words of advice from the navigator.

The Austrian racer Jochen Rindt sits in his car, ready to begin at the starting signal.

88

At the starting line, the driver tenses as he looks at the other racers.

Congratulations for the winners at the end of the race.

89

of the nine races which counted, Brabham won six with a Cooper.

The two drivers that dominated the 1960 season were Brabham and New Zealander Bruce McLaren. Both won six of the nine races with Coopers. Brabham was the champion again that year.

1961 was a year of glory for the Ferrari car. One of its drivers, Phil Hill, was champion, while Von Tripps, also in a Ferrari, came in second. Moss, as in the past season, finished third.

In 1962, Graham Hill won the races of South Africa, Germany, Holland, and Italy with a BRM, and was champion. The Scotsman Jim Clark won his first three Grand Prix races with a Lotus and finished 12 points behind Graham Hill.

Jim Clark won his first championship in 1963, winning seven races, two of them with a BRM. Thanks to the points he accumulated, John Surtees was the champion of 1964, having won only two races, while Graham Hill also won two but finished second. Jim Clark, who won three, finished third.

The second championship that Clark won was in 1965, with six races. Hill was the runner-up with two victories, and in third place was another Scotsman, Jackie Stewart.

Jack Brabham, who was champion in 1959 and 1960, gained his third title in 1966, but this time he raced his own cars, Brabham-Repco, instead of the Coopers that he drove in previous years. Surtees, in the last year that he drove Ferraris, was second and a young Austrian, Jochen Rindt, was third.

Dennis Hulme, another New Zealander who drives Brabhams, won the 1967 title, followed by his patron, Brabham. Clark, who won more races than anyone else (four), finished third.

Graham Hill, who was second in the 1964 competition, won the 1968 championship with a Lotus. In 1969, Jackie Stewart clinched the title even before all the races were run by winning the first six. Jochen Rindt posthumously won the 1970 championship. He was killed during a practice race for the 1970 Italian Grand Prix at Monza.

Stirling Moss before the start of a race. He is probably reviewing the manoeuvres he will make at different points on the track.

Graham Hill, twice World Driving Champion, in a Formula 1 Ford Lotus.

THE DRIVERS

Auto racing is a unique sport. In most other competitive events, you form part of a team, or win a championship for your country. In auto racing, however, you are an individual racing for recognition for yourself. You might be a member of the driving team for a certain type of car—but whenever you win a race, no matter what car you are driving or what country

An accident at the Mexican Grand Prix: Dennis Hulme's car caught fire, but the driver was saved.

Jacki Ickx of Belgium driving a Ferrari.

you are from, *you* get the points that contribute to a championship.

Racing drivers are an unusual breed of men. They are strong—and not just physically. Frenchman Jean-Pierre Betoise was involved in a serious accident at Rheims, France, in 1964. He lost the use of his left arm and leg. But thanks to his stubborn streak, he recovered enough so that he now leads a team of drivers for the French Matra automobile.

Of course, being physically fit is important also. The effort of driving for hours and hours, plus the alertness necessary to make quick decisions and sudden moves, demands that a driver live and breathe cars. Racing cars—if it is to be taken seriously—is not just a Sunday sport.

Some drivers have become so involved with car racing that they have designed their own cars. Jack Brabham, an Australian driver who was World Champion in 1959, 1960 and 1966, designed and raced his own car, the Brabham. In fact, Brabham made racing history by being the first driver to win the World Championship (in 1966) in a car of his own manufacture.

Dan Gurney, an American, raced in many cars—Ferrari, BRM, Porsche, Brabham—until he too designed and raced his own, the Eagle. While he never won the World Championship, his car did quite well nevertheless: at Indianapolis in 1968,

Gurney was second behind another Eagle driven by American Bobby Unser; in 1969, he was second; and in 1970, in a new dart-shaped Eagle, third.

Another driver whose life was very much affected by this sport was Sir Henry Seagrave, an Englishman, who was one of the first racing drivers. Seagrave was knighted for his racing achievements. And John Surtees, also British, was so interested in racing that, after he won the World Championship in motorcycle racing seven times, he changed to cars. He became World Champion in car racing in 1964—the only person ever to hold the title in both cars and motorcycles.

But don't let these success stories fool you into thinking that auto racing is a glamorous sport. Everyone involved agrees that it is as dangerous as can be, and a driver never knows if he will safely complete a race. High speeds, sharp curves, many competitors—these things make a race exciting, but they also make it dangerous.

Although unidentifiable in this picture, the driver is Jackie Stewart of England.

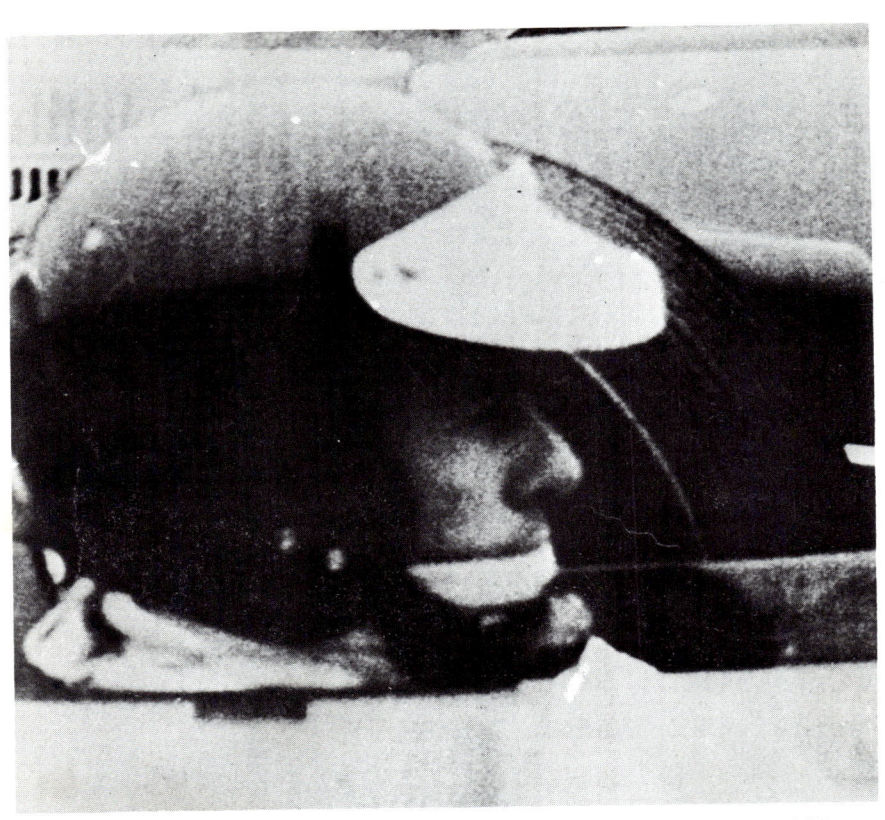

Jim Clark, who was World Driving Champion in 1963 and 1965, was photographed five laps before the crash that cost his life in a Formula 2 trial.

Probably the most famous crash was the one in which Jim Clark, the 1963 and 1965 World Champion, was killed. In April, 1968, Scotsman Clark was racing in an unimportant Formula 2 race in Hockenheim, Germany when, it is reported, he swerved to avoid some children crossing the track and was killed.

New Zealander Bruce McLaren and Britisher Peter Collins are two more drivers killed while racing. Collins crashed in the 1958 German Grand Prix at Nürburgring, while McLaren was killed while testing a new car in 1970. McLaren had been the youngest driver ever to win a Formula 1 World Champion race—at 22, he won the 1959 United States Grand Prix, at Sebring.

An excellent British driver who, because of the point system,

Victorious Jim Clark waves after a long race.

never won the World Championship, Stirling Moss retired in 1962 after a near-fatal accident at Goodwood, England. Jackie Stewart was also involved in a serious accident, in the 1966 Belgian Grand Prix. Since then he has continued racing, but he has also concerned himself with the safety aspects of this dangerous sport. His recommendations have been controversial, but they have ultimately saved lives.

Another way in which racing is a different sort of sport is that the age of the driver is not such an important factor. As long as he is physically fit, he can be as young as New Zealander Chris Amon, who at 19 was the youngest driver ever to race in a Grand Prix race; or as old as Juan Manuel Fangio, who finally retired in 1958 at the age of 47, after winning five World Championships—the last one in 1957!

While drivers are not necessarily the same age, however, they are usually from the same economic background—that is, wealthy. Buying one-of-a-kind racing cars costs money, as does

Jim Clark's car after his fatal crash in 1968.

Completely surrounded by either the car's safety features or his crash helmet and goggles, a driver is protected with the most modern plastics. Further improvements in safety are being made every year.

repairing and tuning them for every race. One exception to this rule is Denny Hulme, a New Zealander now living in Britain. Hulme won a trip to England in 1960 to represent New Zealand in some races, and stayed there by joining Jack Brabham's team as a mechanic. Beginning with Formula Junior races, Hulme climbed upward until he was competing in Formula 1 races in

1966—and won the World Championship in 1967. Hulme's story should give hope to aspiring drivers who are less than rich.

Graham Hill also got his start in racing by working as a mechanic, for the Lotus team. He drove for Lotus in the Formula 1 Grands Prix in 1958, and joined the BRM team in 1960. He won his first World Championship in 1962 in a BRM, and his second in 1968. Living in London, Hill's hobby—when racing leaves him time—is a Piper Aztec plane, bought with the prize money from the 1966 Indianapolis 500.

If you are interested in racing, you must go through the proper channels in your country. In Britain, contact the Royal Automobile Club to obtain a special competition license and a list of other regulations. In the United States, the Sports Car Club of America will inform you of the rules.

Graham Hill is ready to race in a Ford Lotus. Virtually every part of his body is protected by safety equipment.

THE MOST FAMOUS CIRCUITS

AVUS

Situated near Berlin, Avus was a very fast and dangerous circuit on which the French driver Jean Behra was killed. It was 12.25 miles long and consisted of two long parallel straightaways, almost together, linked by a small curve on the south, and by a wider, banked curve on the north. When Berlin was divided, part of the south zone of the track was on the Soviet side, making a shorter circuit only 5.16 miles. The last race in Avus, for cars of Formula 1, was in 1959. Fangio holds the circuit record by racing a Mercedes of Formula 1 at 137.5 mph.

BRANDS HATCH

Located on the outskirts of London, the Brands Hatch circuit was used after World War II. Little by little, it was improved and rearranged until the British Grand Prix was raced there in 1964 and again in 1966.

Only 2.65 miles, the circuit has several curves and grades that give it a lot of interest. Brabham holds the speed record here with a Brabham-Repco of Formula 1, by driving at 97.5 mph to complete the circuit in 1 min. 37 sec.

BRANDS HATCH

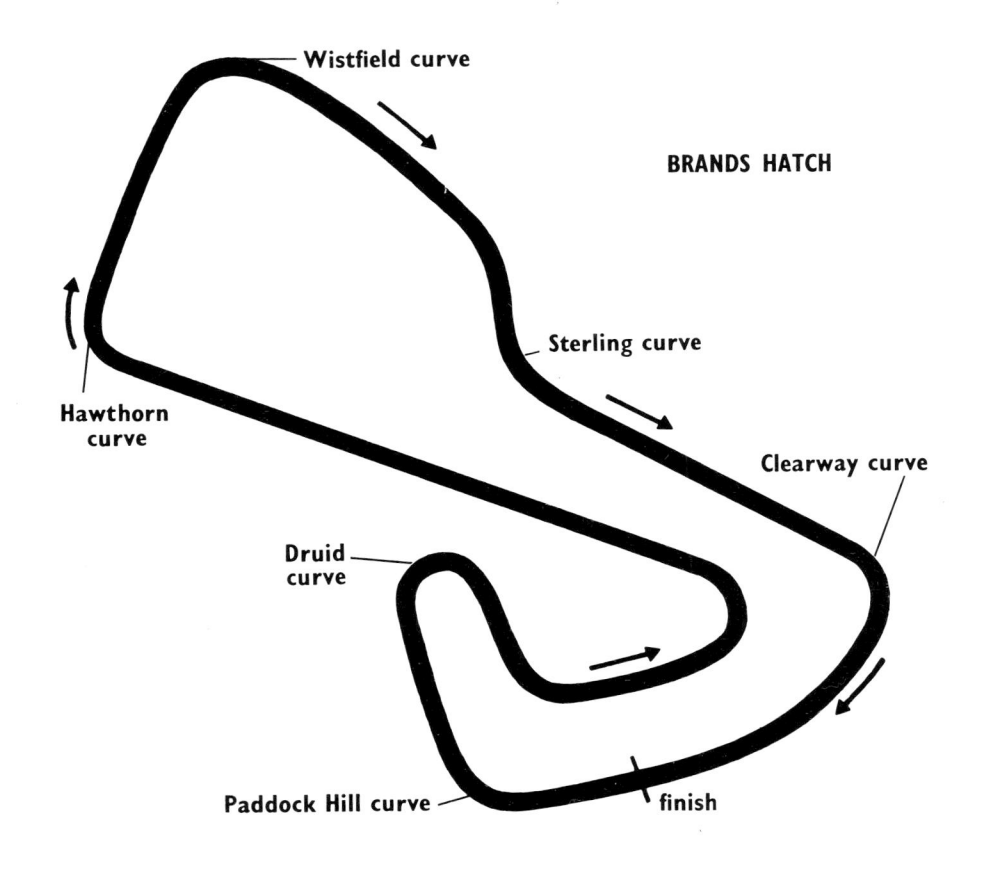

- Wistfield curve
- Hawthorn curve
- Sterling curve
- Clearway curve
- Druid curve
- Paddock Hill curve
- finish

LE MANS

This circuit is formed by the highways that go from Le Mans to Laigne-en-Belin to Mulsanne, in France. Through its history the route has had some modifications in its layout, and it is now 8.36 miles long.

The start is at the end of a straightaway, among the stands and pits. The course very quickly turns into a curving, up-and-down path that alternates with brief stretches of straightaway. After several dangerous curves comes a 2-mile-long straightaway, where the drivers go as fast as they can. At the end of this straightaway is the difficult, closed curve of Mulsanne. Right after this are the signalling pits, since it is only here that the drivers travel slowly enough to read the signs. Next come two very open curves to the right, and then an S-curve called the Arnage curve. Some open curves lie along the highway between

Le Mans and Laigne-en-Belin, and after the White House curve is the judges' straightaway. In 1967, to reduce speed along this stretch, an artificial deacceleration curve called the Ford curve was plotted.

The track record is held by Mario Andretti and Dennis Hulme, who drove a Ford MK IV over the track in 3 min. 23.6 sec., at an average speed of 147.6 mph.

MONACO

The Monaco Grand Prix is run through the streets of Monte Carlo, the capital of Monaco. It is a difficult, winding circuit, with uneven stretches and very short straightaways that make this a true test—not only for the drivers, but also for the cars' transmissions.

It is 1.95 miles long. The starting and finish line is located almost at the end of the boulevard that is at the bottom of the port; soon after this is a hairpin curve to the right; then the track continues on the other side of the boulevard, with the pits in the middle. At the end is a curve of almost 90° that climbs up a hill. Next, a turn to the left, followed by another to the right, where the Casino Plaza is located. From here begins a curved

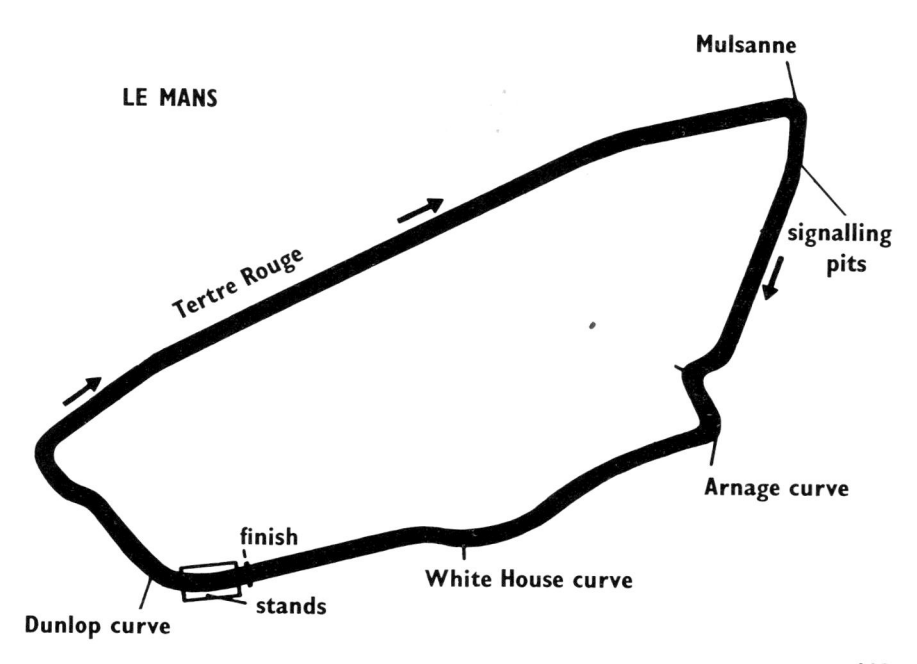

LE MANS

Mulsanne
signalling pits
Tertre Rouge
Arnage curve
finish
stands
White House curve
Dunlop curve

downgrade to the ocean. In the middle of a very open curve, the route goes under a tunnel and comes out into a stretch that is almost straight and leads to the port. After going over this side of the pier, there is a 90° curve to the left that opens onto the boulevard where the finish line is.

Fagiolo (1952) and Bandini (1967) have died on this circuit. The speed record is held by Jochen Rindt, who averaged 81.84 mph in his Lotus.

MONZA

This race track, built inside a park near Milan, is considered to be very fast, and safe for the spectators. It has a drawback for the public, though: it is visible on only a small part of its course. Its peculiar layout lets it be used either in the form of a "boomerang" or a high speed ring, or the two together.

In the main straightaway is the starting and finish line, between the main stand and the pits. At the end of the straightaway, the course feeds into a very open curve, called the Grand·curve; then there is an almost straight stretch with a very open curve in the center called della Roggia. Now comes the short end of the

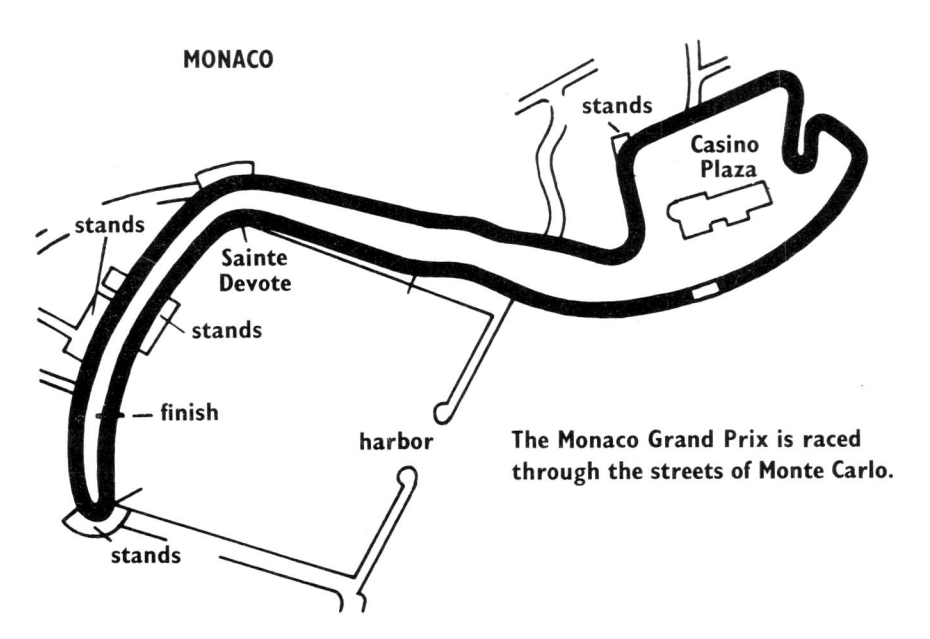

The Monaco Grand Prix is raced through the streets of Monte Carlo.

MONZA

The boomerang and ring of the Monza track.

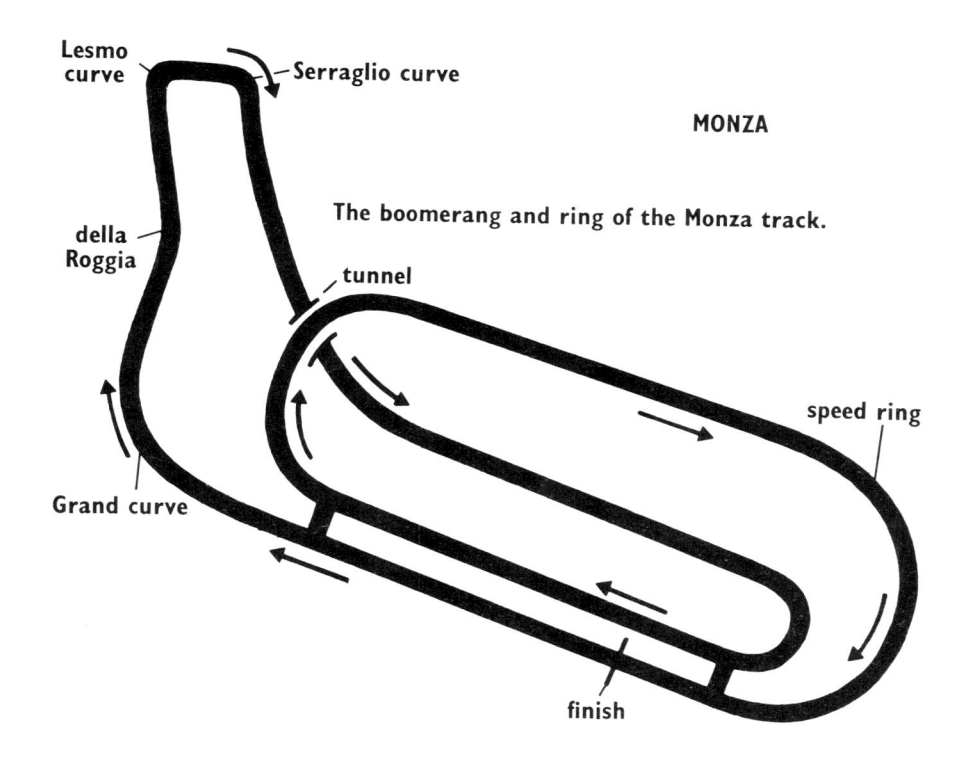

boomerang, called the Lesmo curve, and then a straight stretch into the small elbow curve, Serraglio. The course passes under the banked north end of the curve, and enters a short straightaway parallel to the stands; through the south curve, it reaches the straightaway of the stands. If the speed ring is included, the circuit approaches the north curve, followed by the east straightaway and the south curve, and then again enters the wide straightaway of the stands. These two curves are banked very steeply, which is hard on the cars.

The length of the "boomerang" is 3.59 miles and with the ring included about 6 miles. Among the most important trials run here are the Italian Grand Prix for Formula 1's and the 1,000 Kilometer (600 miles) of Monza for Sport-Prototypes.

Clay Regazzoni was the winning driver at Monza in the 1970 Italian Grand Prix, averaging 147.93 mph.

NURBURGRING

Situated in the Eifel Mountains near Bonn, Germany, the Nürburgring circuit—reputed to be the most beautiful and the most difficult—surrounds the Nürburg castle on a hill in a medieval landscape. It has 174 curves.

The start is on a straightaway in the south end of the circuit. Through a hairpin curve, the course enters into another straightaway that runs parallel to the stands, separated only by the pits; through the Hatzenbach curve the course enters into a winding highway. The length of the circuit is 14.2 miles. Besides the German Grand Prix, the Nürburgring track is also used for the ADAC 1,000-Kilometer for Sport-Prototype cars.

SEBRING

Sebring, Florida is the setting of the famous 12 Hours, which was run for the first time in 1952, and which since 1954 has counted for the Manufacturers' Championship of Sport-Prototype cars. This 5.20-mile circuit is situated on a practically abandoned airfield. The starting and finish line are on a straight-

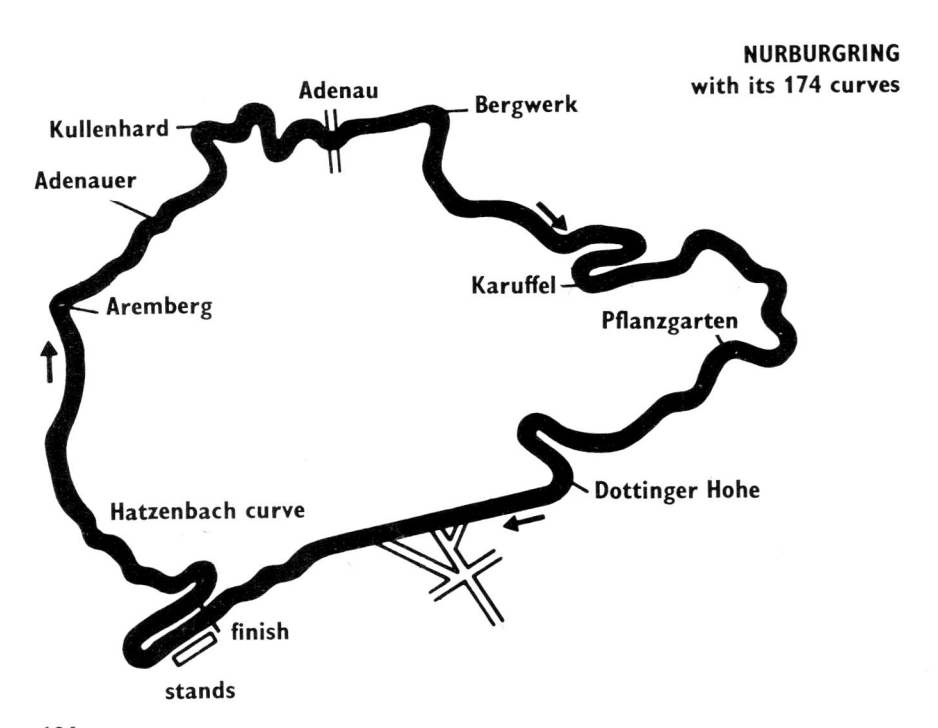

NURBURGRING with its 174 curves

Kullenhard
Adenauer
Adenau
Bergwerk
Aremberg
Karuffel
Pflanzgarten
Hatzenbach curve
Dottinger Hohe
finish
stands

106

SEBRING

Warehouse straightaway
S-curves
Tower curve
Hairpin curve
stands
finish
Backstretch straightaway

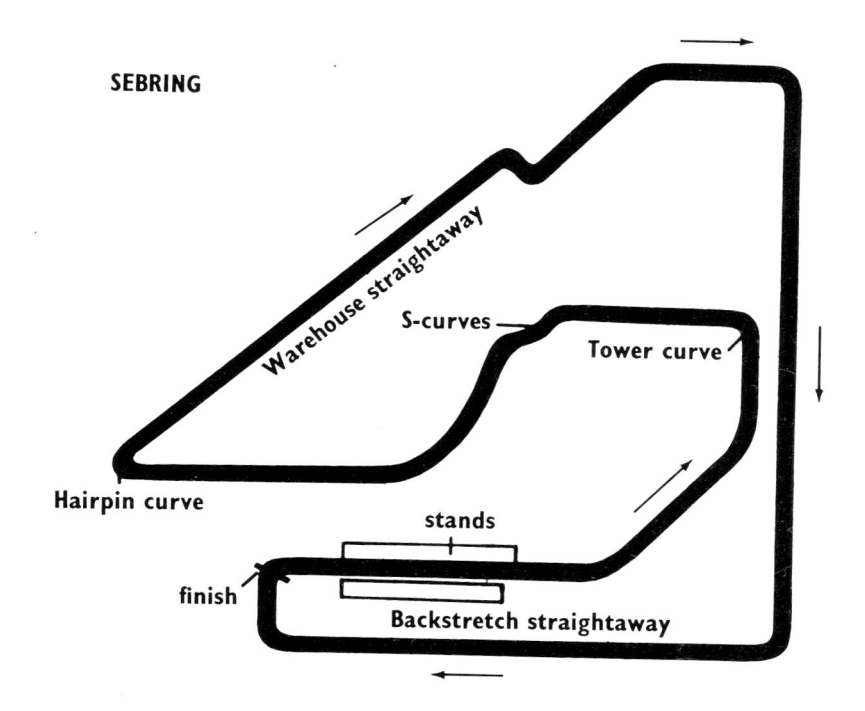

away between the stands and the pits, between the Martini Rossi and Mercedes-Benz bridges. This straightaway is about a third of a mile long, and after a curve to the left the course enters into another straightaway of almost .2 miles. Then comes another curve of about 135°, and another straight stretch of a little more than .1 miles. At the 90° curve called the Tower curve the cement pavement ends and the track becomes asphalt, with a very short straightaway that finishes at a bridge. Right after this are the S-curves, followed by a very wide curve that ends in a straightaway of almost .6 miles. After the Hairpin curve is the Warehouse straightaway, a little more than .6 miles that finishes in another straightaway called Boulevard of Green Park, again on concrete. From the north end of the circuit into a right-angle curve, the course enters onto a mile-long straightaway that runs north-south. Finally, there is another right-angle curve to the Backstretch straightaway of more than half a mile, parallel to the straightaway by the stands, which is reached after a U-curve.

SPA-FRANCORCHAMPS

Located in Belgium between Spa and Francorchamps, this circuit is very long—8.76 miles—and one of the fastest. It is a peculiar location for a track, because the climate is always unstable and it is rare when a torrential rain does not fall on all or part of the track. The race starts near the north end of the track, and at the end of a downgrade is a curve called "L'eau Rouge." The curve of Burneville is one of the sharp angles in this circuit, which is shaped like a triangle. On the side going south are the famous sharp curves of Malmedy and Masta. The extreme south end is formed by the closed curve of Stavelot; on the latter part of the curve, the track is already going north. On the longer side of the triangle are the curves of La Carriere and Blanchimont. Then comes the closed hairpin of La Source at the extreme north, only a few yards from the finish.

This circuit is used for the Belgian Grand Prix of Formula 1 cars, the 1,000-Kilometer of Spa for Sport-Prototypes, and the 24 Hours for Touring Cars. Pedro Rodriguez zipped over this circuit to win the 1970 Belgian Grand Prix at 149.61 mph.

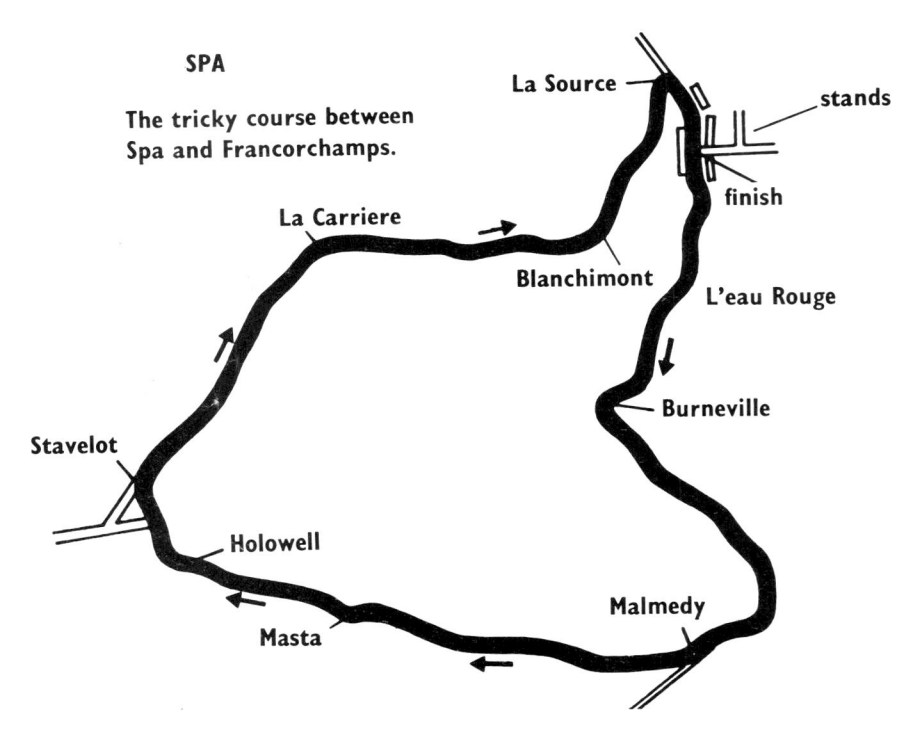

SPA

The tricky course between Spa and Francorchamps.

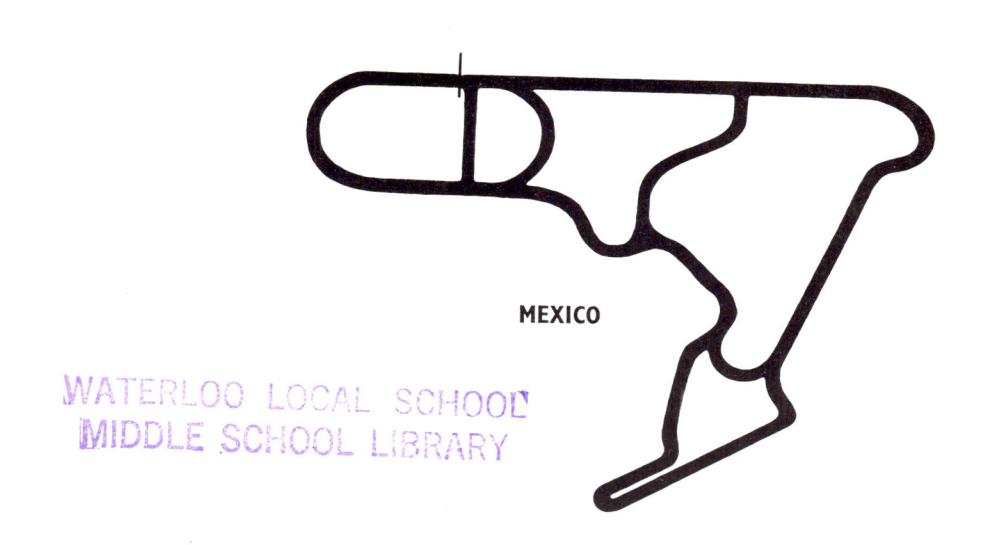

MEXICO

RIVERSIDE

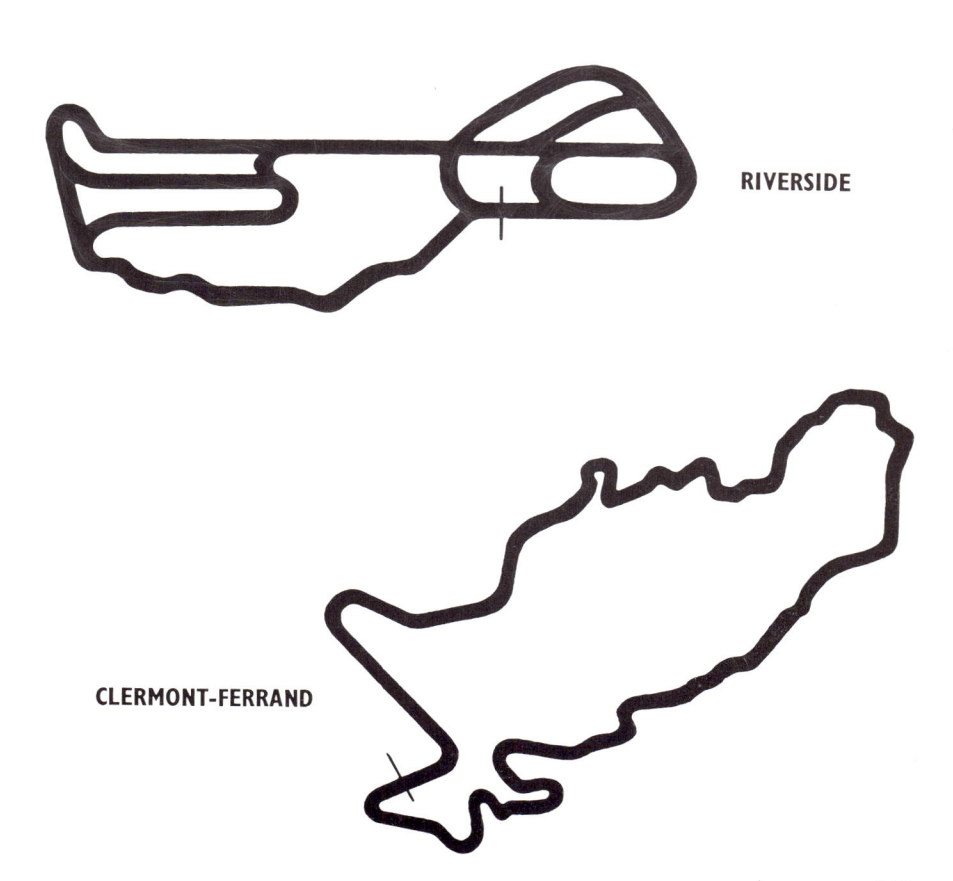

CLERMONT-FERRAND

DAYTONA

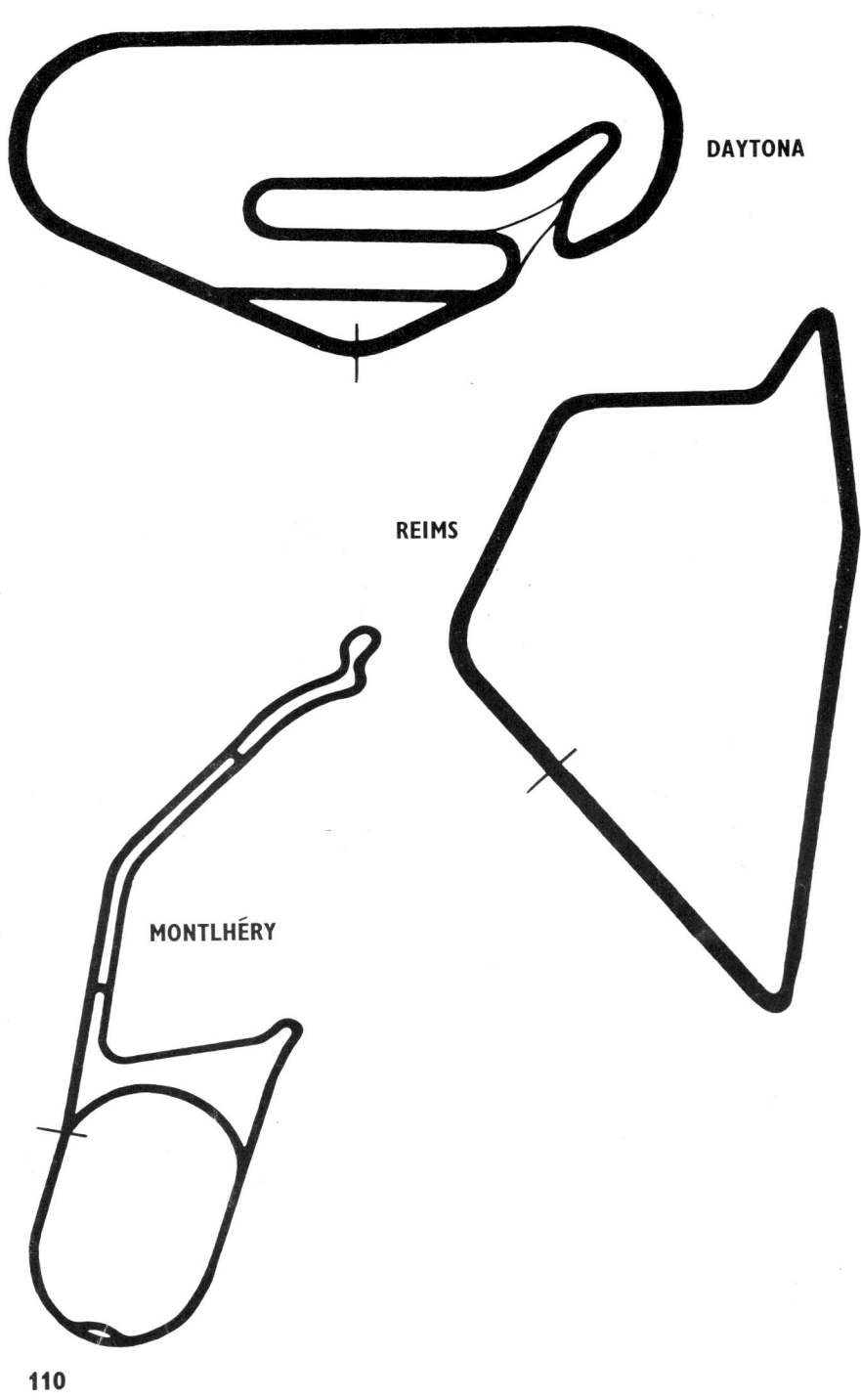

REIMS

MONTLHÉRY

110

SILVERSTONE

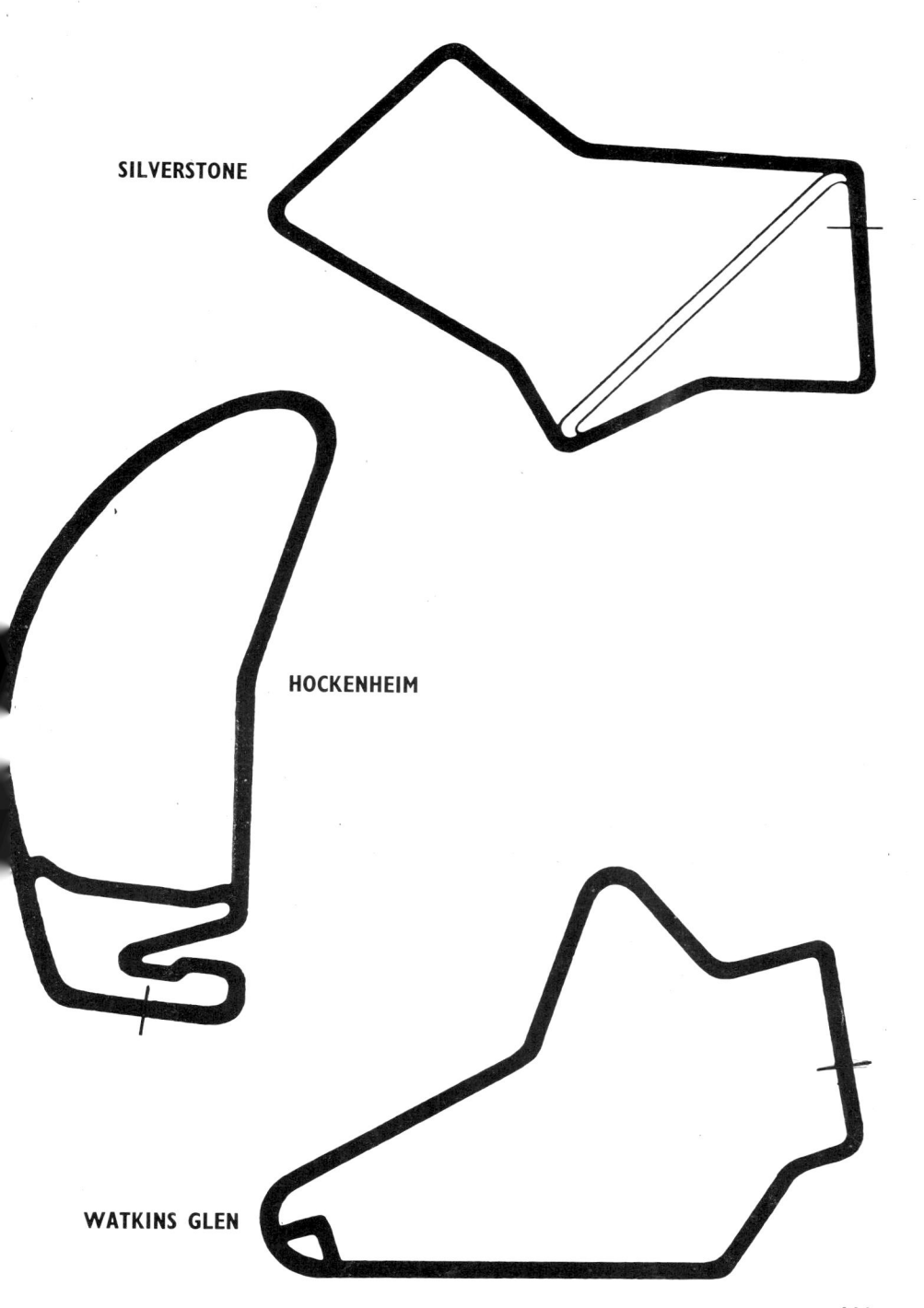

HOCKENHEIM

WATKINS GLEN

Index

aileron, 56–57
air-cooled engine, 46
alternator, 44
Amon, Chris, 98
Andretti, Mario, 103
Ascari, Alberto, 86
Automobile Club of France, 16
Avus, 101
battery, 44
Benz, Carl, 11, 12, 71
Benz-Dreirad, 11
Betoise, Jean-Pierre, 94
"Birdcage," 55
Blitzen-Benz, 13
Bluebird, 23, 24
body, 56–57
Bollée, Amédée, 7
Bouton, 14, 15
Brabham car, 60, 94
Brabham, Jack, 60, 63, 87–90, 94, 101
Brands Hatch, 101–102
brakes, 51–52
Breedlove, Craig, 25
BRM, 60–61
Campbell, Donald, 24
Campbell, Malcolm, 22–24
Camshaft, 43
Canadian American Challenge Cup, 66
CanAm, 66, 70
Chaparral, 62–63
carburetor, 40–41
chassis, 54–55
chevaux-vapeur, 38–39
Clark, Jim, 90, 96, 97–98
Clermont-Ferrand, 109
clutch, 47–48
competition cars, 26–31
compression ratio, 41
compression stroke, 34–35
condenser, 44
convertible, 57
cooling system, 46–47
Cooper, 63
coupe, 57
CUNA, 38
cylinders, 32–35
Daimler, Gottlieb, 8, 9, 11–12, 71
Daytona 24 Hours, 66, 73, 110
De Dion steam car, 14, 15, 16
Deutz Motor Factory, 9–11
differential, 50–51
DIN, 38
disc brake, 52
displacement, 32–33
distribution, 44
drum brake, 51–52
dry pan system, 45
Eagle, 64, 94
electrical system, 44
electric car, 8, 19
engine, 32–48
engine placement, 37
engine's power, 38–39
ERA, 64

exhaust stroke, 34–35
Fangio, Juan Manuel, 86–87, 98, 101
Ferrari car, 64–66
Ferrari, Enzo, 64
FIA, 26
flags, 84–85
flying start, 82
Ford car, 20–21, 66–67
Ford, Henry, 17–18, 66–67
formula cars, 28–30
four-stroke engine, 35
fuel injection, 41–42
generator, 44
grand touring cars, 28
Gurney, Dan, 64, 94
Hawthorn, Mike, 87
hill climbs, 78–79
Hill, Graham, 62, 90, 92, 100
Hockenheim, 111
horsepower, 38–39
Hulme, Denny, 60, 90, 93, 99, 103
hydraulic shock absorber, 58
ignition, 44
ignition by magneto, 14
ignition stroke, 34–35
Indianapolis 500, 64
intake stroke, 34–35
internal combustion engine, 9–12, 32–48
International Kart Federation, 31
Jaguar, 67–69
Jenatzy, Camille, 8, 19
kart, 31
"La Jamais Contente," 19
laminated leaf spring, 57–58
landaulet, 57
leaf spring, 57–58
Le Mans start, 83
Le Mans 24 Hours, 64, 66, 67, 69, 73, 102–103
Levassor, Emile, 12, 16
limousine, 57
liquid cooling system, 46–47
Lotus, 69–70
lubrication, 45–46
March, 70
Maybach, Wilhelm, 10–12
McLaren, Bruce, 70, 90, 96
McLaren car, 70
measurements of power of engine, 38–39
Mercedes, 21
Mercedes-Benz, 71
Mexico, 109
Model T Ford, 18
Monaco, 103–104
monocoque chassis, 55
Monte Carlo, 103–104
Monza, 5, 63, 66, 74, 90, 104–105
Montlhéry, 110
Moss, Stirling, 87, 90, 91, 98
motor brake, 51
Nürburgring, 64, 66, 73, 74, 96, 106
oil, 45
Otto, Nicholas August, 9–10
overdrive, 50

overhead valves, 43
piston rings, 45
placement of engine, 37
Porsche car, 70, 71, 72–74
Porsche, Ferdinand, 8, 72
power of engine, 38–39
rallies, 76–78
rear-wheel drive, 51
Reims, 110
Rindt, Jochen, 88, 90, 104
Riverside, 109
roadster, 57
rotary engine, 35–36
Royal Automobile Club, 100
rpm, 35
SAE, 38
"scratch," 76, 78
Seagrave, Sir Henry, 22–23, 95
Sebring 12 Hours, 64, 73, 74, 106–107
sedan, 57
sedan de ville, 57
shock absorbers, 58
side valves, 43
Silverstone 111
single-seater racing cars, 28–30
single shell chassis, 55
Spa-Francorchamps, 108
spark plug, 44
special touring cars, 28
speed races, 80–85
speed records, 19–25
Sports Car Club of America, 100
sports cars, 28
sports-prototype cars, 28
sports trials, 76–85
springs, 57
standard touring cars, 27
station wagon, 57
steam engine, 6–7, 19, 21
steering, 53
Stewart, Jackie, 70, 75, 90, 95, 98
Summers, Bob, 24
superchargers, 42
Surtees, John, 90, 95
suspension, 57–59
third gear, 50
Thunderbolt, 24
tires, 16
torsion bar, 57–58
touring cars, 27
transmission, 49–50
tubular chassis, 55
two-seater racing cars, 28
two-stroke engine, 33–35
Unser, Bobby, 95
valves, 43
viscosity of oil, 45
Wankel rotary engine, 35–36
Watkins, Glen, 111
wheels, development of, 16
World Championship of Drivers, 86–91
World Sports Car Manufacturers' Championship, 74
X chassis, 54

112

Here Is Your Hobby

Motorcycling

About the Book

Man-made mechanical beasts seem to be more difficult for man to tame than the beasts of the forests. And the motorcycle is one mechanical marvel that sorely needs to be tamed. Two-wheeled vehicles provide sport, inexpensive transportation, and many opportunities for social outings. But all these benefits come only to the rider who knows and masters his machine, who can ride it in safety and keep it in efficient operating condition.

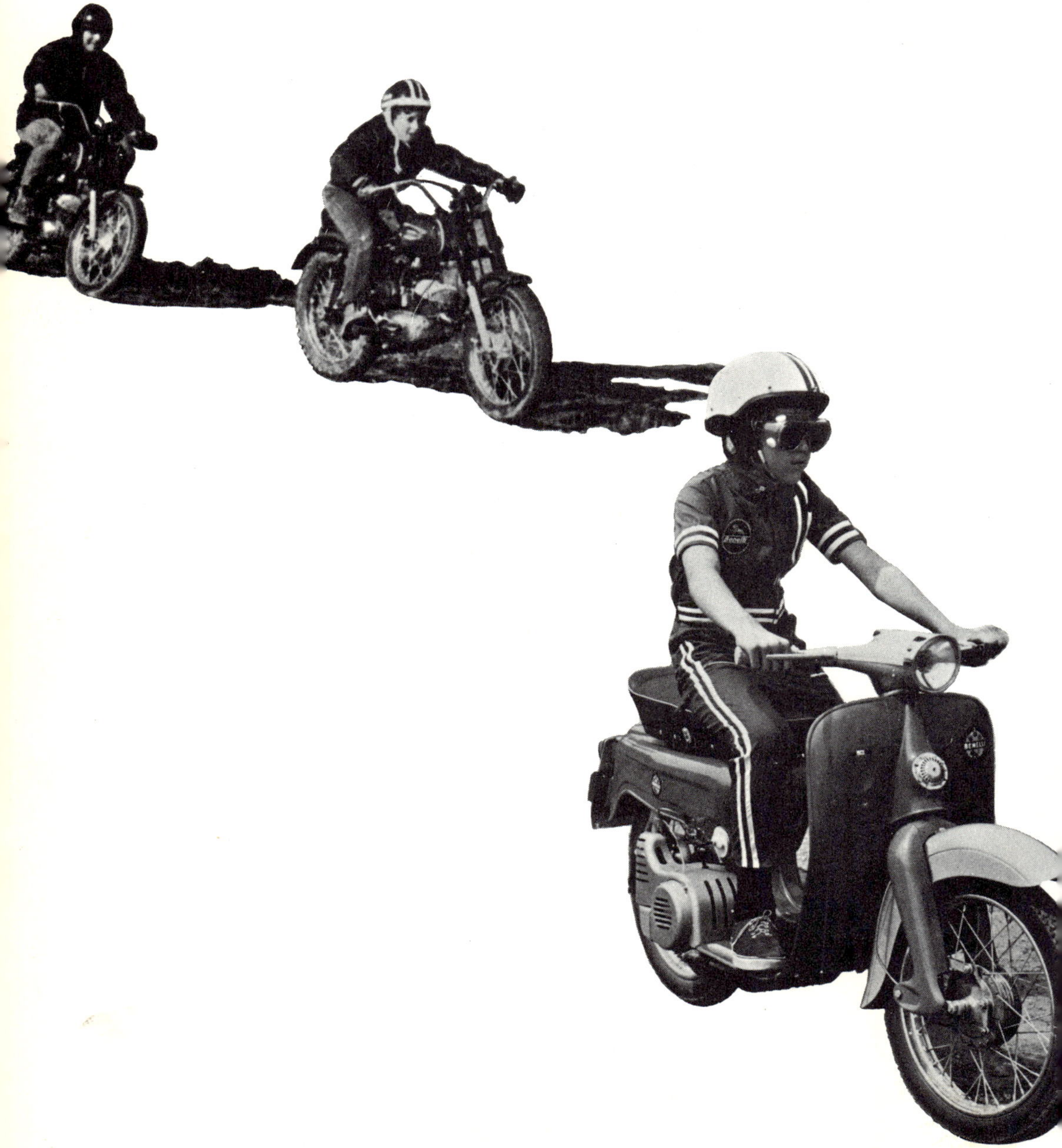

HERE IS YOUR HOBBY...

Motorcycling

A 29 2

by Charles Yerkow

G. P. Putnam's Sons   New York

Dedicated to

Manuel "Spags" Gonzales

Fourth Impression

Copyright © 1973 by Charles Yerkow

All rights reserved. Published simultaneously in
Canada by Longman Canada Limited, Toronto.
SBN: GB-399-60820-6
SBN: TR-399-20331-1

Library of Congress Catalog Card Number: 72-76740

PRINTED IN THE UNITED STATES OF AMERICA
12216

Contents

1 Which Two-wheeler for You? **9**
2 Learning to Ride **37**
3 Buying Your First Motorcycle **59**
4 Riding in Traffic **67**
5 Techniques and Skill **79**
6 Maintenance and Troubleshooting **105**
7 The Motorcycle's Family Tree **115**
Index **123**

Acknowledgments

A book of this kind would not be possible without the willing cooperation of many motorcycling enthusiasts, and to these I am grateful for the technical information and other assistance they gave.

Special thanks to Tom Washburn and his son, Tommy; to Don Carlson and his sons, Bruce and Brian, and his daughter, Janice; to the staff at American Jawa—V. Jarolim, T. Burke, J. Tucek, J. Mendlovsky, and M. Halm; to the staff at Cosmopolitan Motors—Ernest and Lawrence Wise, Joseph Rottigni, Larry Young, Paul Miller, and Michael Hunn; to Emmett Moore of Eastern Kawasaki Motorcycle Corp.; to R. D. Rockwood of Yamaha International; to Stanley Bogan of BSA; to American Honda Motors; to Suzuki Motor Corp.; to riders Frank Sloan and James Cooke; and for specific technical information Don Whyte and Phil Smith.

CHARLES YERKOW

Here Is Your Hobby

Motorcycling

To enjoy the sport of motorcycling, the rider must know his machine—and know how to handle it under all conditions.

1 Which Two-wheeler for You?

So you're ready to join the millions of riders who prefer a motorcycle to a sports car or a sedan. You're joining a new breed of adventuresome, fun-loving people. Tooling along a highway, purring through a city street, or bulling up a mountain, the motorcyclist is an independent character who loves to ride. He is proud of his riding skill and devoted to his machine.

Before you don goggles and gloves, you should learn something about motorcycles and the engines that make them go. Riding a motorcycle calls for technical knowledge as well as physical ability. This book is meant to be your guide to understanding motorcycles and to becoming a safe, skillful rider—and doing it without a spill.

The first step to competent riding is learning how a motorcycle works. Start by comparing it to a bicycle. The first bicycle was merely pushed along. It had no means of power; it was impractical, a luxury. But when pedals were fitted and a chain hooked over the rear-wheel sprocket, the invention became practical and thousands of people began to use it for fun and transportation.

The bicycle became a motorcycle when a small engine was installed in the frame. With engine power the two-wheeler was able to go virtually anywhere, even where no roads ex-

Weighing only 150 pounds, the Benelli Monaco scooter with large wheels can easily double for transportation and fun riding. Engine is a single-cylinder 125-cc, with a three-speed gearbox.

The Jawa Tatran uses a 125-cc single-cylinder two-stroke engine and four-speed gearbox. With its streamlined shroud, lockable battery and tool compartment, and comfortable seat for two, this 250-pound scooter is ideal for short trips or leisurely touring. Note full cover for chain and directional lights.

Reliable single-cylinder 50-cc engines power the lightweight large-wheel scooter (*left*) and motorcycle (*right*), both Jawa models.

isted. Motorcycle riders began exploring faraway places. They raced each other, or they simply used their vehicles for cheap transportation.

The basic concept of a small engine in a frame mounted on two wheels did not change through the years. It's true that the whole machine and its many components underwent countless experiments, all for overall improvements, but in principle the motorcycle remained the same.

Here is a brief view of the kinds of two-wheelers you'll see in the streets and on the roads.

Moped (motor and pedals)

A small-engine combination bicycle and motorcycle. This moped is very popular throughout Europe, and occasionally you will see it in big American cities. The moped uses pedals to start up the engine and to help it along on steeper hills. On level ground the machine runs nicely and fairly fast. It uses little fuel and is so light you can carry it into a basement or an apartment. The engine on a moped may be mounted over the front wheel, at the pedals, or inside the rear wheel.

Scooter

Heavier than a moped, the scooter uses an engine of from 5 to 7 horsepower and will cruise at 35, 45 and even 55 miles

The compact 89-pound Benelli Buzzer minicycle is powered by a 65-cc two-stroke engine and four-speed gearbox. (Cosmopolitan Motors)

per hour, depending on the model. Some years ago in America the scooter proved itself an economical and practical means of transportation in cities and in suburban areas. Whether they worked with a full clutch and a set of gears or the automatic-type clutch, scooters were a dream for many people. The most popular were the small-wheeled Italian Lambretta and Vespa models, with completely trouble-free engines. Even today New York City policemen use them for patrolling the streets and avenues (but ride much more powerful machines for highway traffic checking).

The larger-wheeled scooter models like the Czechoslovak Jawa Tatran and Italian Benelli Monaco perform almost as a lightweight motorcycle. Both models use a 125-cc engine, regular clutch and gearbox, and both have exceptionally comfortable seats for two. You'll find mopeds and scooters fully equipped with fenders, lights, horn, full frontal and bottom shielding against dirt and rain, and even electric starters, directional light signals, and glove boxes.

Minibikes and Minicyles

These bikes have captured the fancy of the public. Both are rugged performers when used for what they were designed— learning to ride, short trips in town, riding the trails, and even herding cattle. The minibike has at most two speeds, no horn and no lights and therefore cannot be licensed for road use. The minicycle is a scaled-down version of a full motorcycle, completely equipped and licensable.

Regular Motorcyles

They are divided into lightweights (anything up to 240 pounds, approximately), medium-weight machines (from 250

With a compact one-wheel trailer hitched up, this 250-cc Jawa is ready for touring with camping equipment. Side lights on trailer provide safety. (*American Jawa*)

A sidecar can be fitted to certain machines to provide comfort for three and room for extra luggage. Note the light on the sidecar wheel fender.

The HS-1 90-cc Yamaha is an excellent street bike, with automatic oil feed for the two-stroke engine and easy-to-service components.

pounds up to 400), and the heavies (running all the way up to 900 pounds!). You'll find the same basic components in all of them, with either more or less sophistication and chrome. Now and then you'll find a comfortable sidecar attached.

The engine on a regular motorcycle, often called a street bike, may have one cylinder, two, three, or even four, and so the power output will be either on the low side, in the mid-range, or on the high-performance side.

For riding in the streets of a busy city a single-cylinder 50-cc model will keep up with the traffic and, what's most important, will be easy to handle. Going up the line, a 90-cc or 125-cc engine will give you more performance in general, but remember that in some instances the 90-cc model will be geared better for faster getaways than one carrying a 125-cc engine.

When it comes to long-distance touring, the machine with greater engine power and weight will give a more comfortable ride than a lightweight model. It also will be capable of sustained high speeds without overworking the engine.

What it all sums up to is that you have to select a motorcycle for your particular needs. You can't have the best of both sides in one machine, and you must therefore try for the happy middle. Try to fit your requirements. If you're planning to use your bike every day for long trips on an expressway, then a 125-cc model is hardly the answer. On the other hand, if most of your riding will be in congested city streets and only an occasional lark in the country, then a heavy monster with a 60-horsepower engine is not too smart either.

When you look into the special competition machines, you'll realize how finely tailored these bikes are for the job they have to do. This is where you meet the fantastic *dragster*, or the hot and lively *scrambler*, or the rugged *motocross* or *enduro* models, the *road racer, trials machine, hill climber, trail bike* and so on. Each shines in its own backyard, and you'd never try running it in another place because you know it would be a washout.

For competition and off-the-road riding neither you nor your machine needs a license, but if you plan to use your machine in the streets and on the roads, then your bike must be registered and you must have an operator's license. What you must know to pass a motorcycle-riding test will be covered in another chapter.

Now before you buy a motorcycle, you should know a little about engines, clutches, gearboxes, rear sprockets, tires, and other things that make one bike do things that another bike can't do. Knowing the simple technical things, you won't find yourself on a trail bike wondering why it can't get up to 90.

The engine is the heart of the motorcycle, and like any heart it works in order that other parts may also work. Every engine consists of a crankcase with one or several cylinders fitted to it either vertically, sideways, or in some slanted position. Inside a cylinder is a piston, and around every piston are several piston rings which make the upper part of the cylinder air-tight. (The cylinder must be air-tight because the piston must compress the fuel mixture so that it can be ignited by the spark plug.) A rod connects the piston to an arm that is part of the crankshaft, located inside the crankcase. In this way, when the engine is running, the piston moves up and down inside the cylinder and the connecting rod turns the crankshaft. And that's all any engine does: It turns a crankshaft, and this turning force is sent through the gearbox and clutch to the rear wheel of a motorcycle.

In a four-stroke engine the piston moves up and down inside the cylinder four times to produce one power stroke. Thus on the first stroke the piston moves down and sucks in the fuel mixture, which consists of one part gas to roughly fifteen parts air; this mixture is drawn through the carburetor and atom-

The Jawa 90-cc Trail model is a rugged machine designed for both street and trail riding. The high exhaust pipe is shielded, and the front fork, handlebars, and gearing fit the purpose of the bike.

Weighing 260 pounds, the CZ Sport 175 (Jawa) is provided with automatic oil feed for its two-stroke one-cylinder engine.

Engine on this M. V. Agusta is a vertical twin four-stroke of 250-cc with a five-speed gearbox and a rocker-type shift on the right side. This model weighs 330 pounds. Note design of seat for two.

ized, or vaporized, for the intake stroke. Then the piston moves upward and compresses the vapor into the top of the cylinder, completing the second stroke. When the fuel mixture is compressed, the ignition system sets off an electrical spark inside the top of the cylinder. The compressed fuel vapor explodes and pushes the piston downward into the third stroke, called the power stroke. Finally the piston moves upward again and exhausts all the burned gasses out of the cylinder.

In order to make these strokes possible on a four-stroke

engine, the cylinder is designed with intake and exhaust valves which open and close as needed for the various strokes.

In a two-stroke engine the piston moves up and down only two times to produce one power stroke. And the cylinder is designed with openings, or ports, which are covered and uncovered by the piston itself as it moves up and down. Thus compression and intake occur on one stroke, and the exhaust takes place as the explosion pushes the piston down into the power stroke. There are no valves that open and close, and therefore there are no rockers, no pushrods, no springs, no valve guides, and no oil pump for the valve gear. The fuel mixture is one of gasoline and oil and either is premixed in the tank by the rider or is fed to the carburetor by an automatic oil feed system. This same mixture is also used to lubricate the crankshaft and connecting-rod parts.

Note a simple fact. The engine with the higher compression ratio (how tightly the piston squeezes the fuel mixture into the top of the cylinder) will usually outperform a similar engine with a lower compression ratio.

The 250-cc BSA Starfire single-cylinder four-stroker is ideal for short or long-distance runs. (*BSA-East*)

The 350-cc Ducati Scrambler four-stroke single features overhead camshaft. (*Premier Motors*)

The 450-cc Honda twin four-stroker features a special exhaust system, overhead cams, tachometer, and directional lights. (*American Honda*)

It is only natural that motorcycle riders have been arguing throughout the years about which type of engine is the best. The only thing that can be said is that they'll go on arguing for many more years. Every rider decides for himself what he likes and why he likes it. Consider:

On a four-stroker you don't have to bother mixing gas and oil (the proportion is about one part oil to twenty parts gas). But then many two-stroke models have automatic oil feed, and some of the toughest motocross machines are two-stroke types and the riders mix their own gas and oil. On a four-stroke you must watch the oil level in the crankcase, while on a two-stroke type this is taken care of by the intake stroke. On a four-stroker valve trouble can be costly, but a two-stroker must be decarbonized every so often. A four-stroker gives better mileage per gallon of gas, but if it's out of tune, you'll have a harder time starting the engine On a two-stroker you don't have to worry about timing the valves and setting the clearances, but during the break-in period of the engine the exhaust will give off telltale gas-oil burning smoke.

And so the arguments go on and on....

When you discuss an engine, you can't help but discuss its size, which means that you're talking about the inside area of the cylinder or cylinders. You simply add up the bore (width of cylinder) and the stroke (length of piston travel), and you state it in cubic centimeter (cc) displacement. When you ask a motorcycle rider what he rides, he'll answer something like this: A Yamaha 250, or a Jawa 350, or a Benelli 125, or a BMW 750. First the name of the bike, then the size of its engine in cubic centimeter displacement. For those who know motorcycles, this much information immediately pegs the machine, and often the rider.

The size of the engine also indicates the approximate power output. A glance at a moped, scooter, or lightweight machine

Machines that run in "motorcross" events must be able to take the toughest terrain and withstand the tremendous shocks and stresses. Like the Bultaco, Husqvarna, and others of its class, this CZ is able to take the punishment. (*Photo by Roy Morsch*)

with one cylinder will tell you that its engine is from 50cc to 125 cc, which can provide about from 4 to 9 horsepower. This power will be good enough to reach top speeds of from 35 to perhaps 55 miles per hour. Remember that this is very good performance from this size engine.

If you have a two-cylinder engine of 200 cc, you actually have two cylinders and each displaces 100 cc. Thus two 175-cc cylinders equal 350 cc. The more cylinders, the smoother the running.

But when it comes to performance, size and power output of the engine are not the whole story. Take two engines of the same size and power, and then change the gearing setup in the gearbox of one, and you'll end up with one performing rings around the other. Go another step and change the rear-wheel sprocket, and you'll again change the performance ability of

Inside this cylinder is a piston and a connecting rod that turns the crankshaft. The gearshift lever is visible at the side of the gearbox. Finning on cylinder is for more efficient air cooling. Note spark plug at top and coil at extreme top left.

the machine. The regular street bikes are designed around a particular engine and gearbox to provide the best performance possible without overstressing the engine or any other part. But when it comes to competition machines, the manufacturer will have a variety of gearing and sprocket arrangements to choose from in order to fit the bike for specialized riding requirements.

The gearbox provides you with a set of gears so that by selecting the right gear, you can start the machine rolling from a standstill, then shift to second gear to gather more speed, then increase the speed with the next gear, and finally use the top gear for cruising speed. The usual arrangement is four gears, but you will find certain models with three gears, and

The valve rockers on a 250-cc M. V. Agusta twin are accessible for adjustment after removing the covers. Each cylinder is fed by a Dell'Orto carb.

others using five, six, or even eight gears. The actual use of gears will be explained later.

When the gearing is "low," it means that the bike has great pulling power but not much in the way of high speed. When the gearing is "high," the bike will be able to reach high speeds but will not get away fast at the light.

The shifting of gears is done by your foot, either the left or right foot, depending on which side the shift lever is located. All gearboxes have a basic neutral position, and many models have additional neutral positions—sometimes as many as there are gears.

Remember one thing about the gears: Always disengage (pull) the clutch first, then shift gears. (On certain Jawa models clutch disengagement is automatic whenever the gearshift lever is moved.)

The clutch is a coupling device between the engine and the

Left-side cover on a 350-cc Jawa twin two-stroker is removed to show the automatic oil feed mechanism, which is controlled by the throttle twist grip.

gears and is made up of either two plates or a set of plates. These plates are forced together by powerful springs inside the clutch housing so that all the plates rotate together when the engine is running. If the gears are in their neutral position, nothing can happen, but if one of the gears has been selected, then the engine will drive the bike. The clutch control lever is always located on the left handlebar. When this lever is pulled or squeezed, the clutch plates are separated (disengaged) and the gears are free to be shifted. When you start releasing the lever, the clutch plates are forced together (engaged) and the bike will start rolling.

The engine, clutch, and gearbox are one unit: The engine produces the turning force, or torque; the gears make it possi-

Gear shifting is done by either right or left foot, depending on the model. On this CZ the lever is lifted up for first gear, then is tapped down for second, third, and fourth gear.

ble to start from a standstill and increase the speed; and the clutch provides the smooth coupling between the engine's crankshaft and the driven gear.

The only step left then is to pass the engine power from the selected gear shaft sprocket to the rear-wheel sprocket, which drives the bike. For this job most machines use a chain, just like the chain on a bicycle, but a few manufacturers (BMW, M. V. Agusta, Moto-Guzzi) equip their machines with a driveshaft to the rear-wheel hub. Both methods serve the same purpose: to drive the rear wheel.

The brakes on most motorcycles are the internal expanding-shoe and drum type, fitted inside the front and rear hub. The front brake is worked by a lever located on the right handlebar,

The chain is the final transmitter of power from the gearbox to the rear-wheel sprocket. Note foot brake pedal ahead of the peg.

Front brake lever on right handlebar and clutch lever on left give rider easy control. The ignition key and speedometer are visible on the headlight of this CZ.

The rear brake pedal is located near foot peg so that foot can easily apply pressure. But foot must not rest on the brake pedal while riding.

and the rear brake is worked by your foot—either left or right, depending on the machine. The two brakes are used together for maximum and equalized braking action. If you're approaching a sharp curve or a corner, use the brakes *before* you start leaning into the turn.

Most machines use the 18-inch-size wheel, and the tires are always selected for the kind of riding to be done. For street and road riding, tires are of a smooth tread design, while those intended for rough terrain use, like enduro and motocross racing, the heavier tread design, called knobbies, are used.

Tire pressure is important. The average machine needs about 22 pounds per square inch (psi) in the front and about

On this Jawa scooter the Barum tires are of a fairly smooth tread design and work well on hard road surfaces and also on trails.

For best traction on rough terrain, heavy cleated or knobby tires are used. Note absence of headlight and the shielded high exhaust pipe.

28 in the rear tire. But pressure needs vary in relation to weather conditions, the road surface, and the load carried. The manufacturer always explains tire pressure requirements in the owner's manual, and smart riders follow the manufacturer's recommendations. A soft tire will give a mushy ride, while a hard one will bounce around too much. In both instances you'll find that the handling characteristics of the bike change for the worse, especially in a curve or where the surface is rough.

Tires naturally cushion the ride, but even so all machines are built with excellent shock-absorbing systems. The front wheel rides in a telescoping set of tubes, with special coil springs and oil-filled chambers, and the rear wheel rides in a swinging arm which is attached to a separate shock-absorbing system. Add to this the cushioned seat or saddle, and the roughest road surface becomes endurable even on long rides.

It is said that most motorcycles are bought because they provide the rider with a feeling of freedom and a sense of power at the twist of the wrist. Maybe they're bought for one more reason—the sound of the exhaust as the engine (often called the mill) begins to rev up.

To a bike buff there is no sweeter sound than a finely tuned engine being put through its paces. At motorcycling meets, engines howl, groan, scream. This is part of the scene as riders and bikes whip across the track or come flying out of gullies. But the same sweet sound has, of course, no meaning other than being a nuisance when heard in a town or city street or on a parkway. There it is hard to take. So the law says, "Don't change the exhaust system of your machine." Some riders think the law is reasonable and they go on enjoying their riding, while others alter their pipes and then complain when the police hand them a summons.

Some exhaust pipes are run under the frame rearward, either in a straight line or with an upsweep. On other models the pipes are midway up, or even way up. It's all a matter of styling, function, and personal preference.

Without the exhaust pipes and the mufflers inside them every explosion inside the cylinder would sound like a rapid-fire cannon. Your job as a motorcycle rider is to create a favorable image for the police and for other users of the road. You can easily do it by not producing roaring and ear-splitting sounds. Remember this: The less noise you make, the more respect you'll get from nonriders!

Before you handle the throttle twist grip on the right handlebar, you should know something about the carburetor. The carburetor (usually called a carb) mixes and atomizes one part gasoline and fifteen parts air and allows the piston to draw this fuel mixture into the cylinder during the intake stroke. As already explained, the spark plug ignites this mixture on the compression stroke.

The carb works in a simple way. When you twist the throttle open (turning the grip counterclockwise), a slide or valve inside the carb opens the passage and lets more fuel vapor through the venturi tube into the cylinder. This speeds up the engine. By completely closing the throttle, the engine will slow down to idling speed.

Every carb is fitted with adjusting screws so that the position of the throttle can be set for best idling and running, and also for setting the best proportion of gas to air. In this way a carb can be set on the rich side (too much gas) or lean side (too much air), depending on the tuning requirements.

The gas flows from the tank to the bowl of the carb. If there's enough gas in the bowl, the float with a shutoff needle will be lifted and the flow of gas will be shut off. As the gas is used from the bowl by the carb, the float and needle will drop and so let more gas into the bowl. This process is continuous as long as the engine is running.

Every carb is fitted with a few devices to make starting easy when the engine is cold. A primer or tickler is a short plunger-like rod which when pressed down forces the float inside the bowl to let in more gas and so flood the carb. This delivers a rich mixture for starting.

Another device is the choke, which comes in many forms, and is used simply to close off the air supply, thus again producing a rich mixture.

To prevent dirt from entering the carb, manufacturers fit special filters to both the fuel inlets and the air induction system. The rider's job thereafter is to make sure these filters are clean.

Once the fuel mixture is drawn into the cylinder, it must be ignited, and this job belongs to the ignition system. There are two types: the magneto (mag) and the battery and coil.

The mag is a self-contained unit consisting of a set of magnets and coils, one or the other rotating. As soon as the engine is kicked over, the magneto produces a powerful spark at the spark plug. In other words, electrical energy here does not depend on a battery. The magneto provides power for ignition, lights and horn. Because competition-type machines do not carry lights and a horn, they use a mag system, saving on weight.

The average motorcycle, however, operates with a battery and coil, which is slightly more complicated and also more bothersome because the battery needs periodic attention to the electrolyte level in the cells. In this system the battery is continually charged by a regulated generator, or an alternator. The system may be a 6-volt or a 12-volt type and will further consist of a set of breaker points and a condenser.

On some motorcycles you will find both a magneto for running the engine and a battery with its generator for the lights and horn. And several models now feature the convenience of

Batteries for motorcycles are either the 6-volt (three cells) or 12-volt (six cells) type, usually fitted under or at the side of the seat.

With right-side cover removed on this 350-cc Jawa, the ignition breaker points and condenser are shown. Clutch cable and automatic clutch mechanism are visible and also the rear brake pedal at the peg.

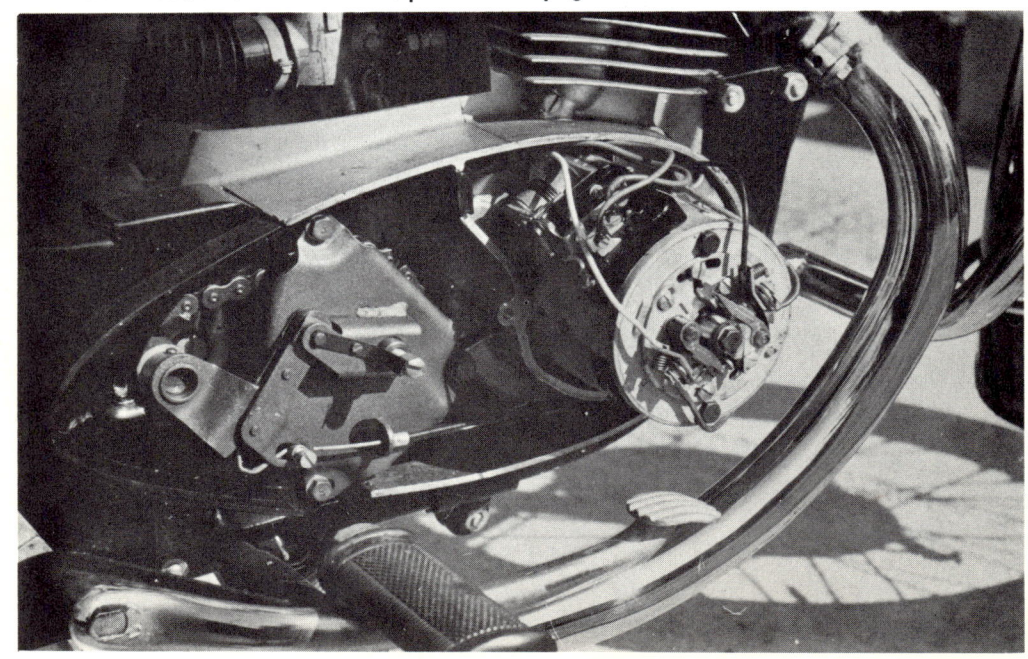

On this CZ model the left-side gearshift lever also acts as a kick starter.

the electric starter, which also draws current from the battery.

The usual engine-starting device, however, is the kick lever. For years this has provided motorcycling enthusiasts with a mixture of satisfaction and utter heartbreak, depending on whether the engine fired up or teased its rider with consistent coughs.

All motorcycles feature a headlight and a taillight and also a stoplight at the rear. Conveniently located switches on the handlebar make it easy for the rider to signal with the horn, raise or lower the headlight beam, and signal left and right turns. A speedometer and sometimes a tachometer are fitted near the headlight (or in it) so that the rider can tell how fast he's traveling and how fast the engine is turning over. On some machines small lights tell the rider whether the gearbox is in neutral, whether the high beam is on, whether the battery is

35

discharging, and whether the oil pump is providing adequate pressure. And on the latest water-cooled Suzuki even a water temperature indicator is featured!

Designers and engineers are constantly striving to give riders efficient machines with all sorts of safety and comfort items. The actual use of these items is up to the individual rider. Chromed bars sticking out just ahead of the engine are called crash bars and are designed to protect the rider and the engine. One rearview mirror on the left side of the handlebar is required by law; another mirror on the right side gives you added safety. A heavy-duty front windshield gives added protection for the eyes, face, and body when loose stones are kicked up by the car in front of you. In cold weather the shield keeps the cold wind from hitting you full force. But on windy days the windshield acts like a sail and has been known to force the bike right off the road—so be careful.

One thing that every rider should carry is a set of tools for making small repairs or adjustments on his bike. A tube patching kit should be part of this equipment, and so should a spare spark plug, chain links, tire pump, set of points, spare taillight, and anything else you think might come in handy when you have a breakdown. Nothing is more exasperating than to have a breakdown on the road and not have the means with which to help yourself.

2 Learning to Ride

Learn to handle a bike before you buy one. No doubt you have a friend who owns one. Perhaps there is an adult in your neighborhood who will let you get the feel of his motorcycle. Maybe he'll even take you for a spin or give you some riding tips.

Get on a motorcycle as soon as possible. Start by getting the feel of the machine without the motor running.

Take hold of the handlebars and push the bike around. Next, roll the bike to a roadway that slopes downhill. This should not be a steep hill, and the road should be lightly traveled.

Don't start up the engine. Just get on the bike, and then let its momentum roll you downhill. Keep your feet on the pegs and your knees against the tank. Remember that your right hand controls the front brake, and your foot (left or right, depending on the model) controls the rear brake. Let the machine roll freely, gathering speed, while you simply ride it the way you would ride a bicycle. If you can ride a bicycle, you can ride a motorcycle.

While rolling downhill, keep the bike heading straight, keep to the right side of the road, and occasionally glance back over your left shoulder. But for the most part keep your eyes front. As you reach the bottom of the hill, begin pressing lightly on the foot brake, and then press harder to bring the bike to a full stop. Then place both feet on the ground, and use the hand brake to keep the machine from rolling.

After rolling downhill several trips, start using both brakes at the same time. You'll be surprised at the stopping power of the brakes when they're used this way. Then, as you're rolling downhill, start practicing gentle swings left and right—just the way you would do it on a bicycle.

Having thus become familiar with the weight and handling of the bike, start up the engine and roll downhill the same way as before. You may even want to blip the engine a few times on your way down. This will test your coordination between handling the machine and the throttle at the same time.

This brings you to the next stage of learning to ride—starting to roll in first gear under power and doing it solo. For this practice you need an empty area on level ground and with virtually no traffic around you.

Pull on your gloves, strap down your helmet, and fit your goggles in place. From now on helmet, goggles, and gloves are a must.

A word of warning: Whether you're a beginner or an experienced rider, *never let anything distract you* when you're operating your motorcycle!

Now that you'll be in charge of a live engine, let's retrace our steps so that you get the whole picture right.

Most likely the machine will be on its center stand, and the engine will be shut off. As a beginner, you should practice starting the engine while the bike is up on the stand because this eliminates the problem of balancing the machine and kicking at the same time (the problem is eliminated if your bike has an electric starter).

Starting up a cold engine can be difficult or it can be easy, depending on how much you know about carburetion and ignition. If the engine is in good mechanical condition, meaning

Before trying to start up the engine, rider checks gas in the tank and opens the fuel valve.

To enrich the fuel mixture for cold weather starting, rider pushes down choke lever, as shown on this Dell'Orto carb, to cut off air supply. Velocity stack is removed to show throttle slide inside carb.

Most carbs have a priming device (tickler) which, when pressed, floods the carb with raw fuel to help start a cold engine. Never press hard against the tickler.

that no part is broken, shafts are not bent, gear teeth are not chewed away, all connections for gas and electrical power are tight, the engine should start after about three kicks of the starter lever.

It should. Sometimes it doesn't, or it may start after twenty kicks, which won't make you happy.

Experienced riders have a way of starting a cold engine, and their system never seems to fail. This is the way it's done:

1. Check the fuel level in the tank, and open the gas line valve underneath the tank to let gas flow into the carb bowl. If the engine you are starting is the two-stroke type with automatic oil feed, check the oil level in the separate oil tank. On a four-stroke engine, check the oil level in the crankcase; on a two-stroke, check the oil level in the gearbox. Gears must be in neutral.

2. If the weather is on the cold side and if your carb is equipped with a choke, set the choke partially or fully closed. This is the way you ensure that the engine will draw in more gas than air, which helps it fire up on the first kick. In warm weather you will not need the choke.
3. Prime the carb by pressing down the tickler or priming rod located on top of the bowl. Press down *gently* for a count of two or three. This floods the carb and ensures a rich mixture for starting.
4. With the ignition still *off*, open the throttle halfway and kick the engine over several times so that the piston draws in the rich mixture. Close the throttle.
5. If the weather is on the warm side, set the ignition *on* and kick the engine over sharply. It should start on the first kick. If the weather is on the cold side, set the ignition *on*, prime the carb once more, and then use the kick starter. Again, the engine should fire up on the first try.

The manner in which you kick against the kick starter is also important because—everything else being equal—this can spell the difference between a start and a no-start.

Position the kick starter lever at the top of its stroke, then bring the lever down slightly with your foot until you feel engine compression. This means the piston inside the cylinder is on the upstroke, compressing the fuel mixture, and just about ready to fire.

Hook your heel into the lever and point your toes down so as not to strike against the peg. Now lift yourself up, hands on the handlebars, and bring your full weight down into the kick. Kick sharply, and kick through—as if you wanted to go clear around the stroke!

If the engine fails to start on the second kick, it will mean poor carburetion (too lean or too rich a mixture) or faulty igni-

Experts begin kick starting with the lever high up, on a compression stroke. Note rider's body weight about to come down onto slightly bent leg.

The kick must be completed to the bottom of the lever's stroke, cleanly and forcefully, and held there for a moment.

tion (loose wires, poor gapping at the spark plug or points). We will discuss troubleshooting and maintenance in another chapter.

Once the engine is running, open the choke partially or fully. In very cold weather keep the choke on for at least one minute. Since motorcycle engines are cooled by air passing over the cylinders, it is not a good idea to stand still too long with a running engine. Play the throttle to keep the engine running, until it warms up. Push the bike off its center stand.

At this stage we will assume that the engine continues to run so that you may start learning how to handle a motorcycle under power. You're in a clear, flat, and traffic-free area, ready to go.

And the going is easy indeed.

1. With both feet on the ground for balance, lean the machine away from the gearshift lever side, all the while holding the front brake on with your right hand. Then with your left hand squeeze the clutch lever on the left handlebar, and hold it squeezed in. The clutch is disengaged.
2. Using your foot, shift into first gear. On most models this gear is one position up from neutral, so that you'll hook your toes under the shift lever and then lift upward until you hear the gear click into position. If your bike has a rocker-type shift lever, then you can press down against the back part of the lever with your heel. Straighten up the bike, both feet on the ground, clutch lever still held squeezed.
3. You are now in gear and ready to move forward. Let go of the front brake lever with your right hand and open the throttle just enough to speed up the engine. Keep both feet on the ground to balance the bike, and then start releasing the clutch—slowly, smoothly. You'll feel

When the clutch lever is pulled, the clutch plates inside the engine housing are disengaged so that rider may shift into gear.

With clutch disengaged, rider can shift gears freely. On this CZ the shift lever is lifted from neutral once for first gear, then is tapped down for higher gears.

The rocker-type gearshift lever on this M. V. Agusta is on the right side of the machine; the heel is used to kick into first gear, then the toe taps forward lever down for higher gears.

    the machine moving forward. The clutch plates are beginning to grab. Continue releasing the clutch all the way, and add just enough engine power to keep rolling. Place both feet on the pegs and ride the bike.

4. After covering a distance of about fifty feet in first gear, disengage the clutch by squeezing the left lever, shut the throttle to idle the engine, and with your foot tap the gearshift lever lightly to get back into neutral position. Release the clutch lever fully.

If you're not sure you have the neutral position, try opening the throttle slightly, very slightly, and if you feel the engine pulling, it means you're still in gear. If this is the case, squeeze the clutch, use the brakes to come to a stop, then shut off the ignition. If, however, you are in neutral, then simply apply the brakes and bring the bike to a stop.

On this Benelli scooter the left hand operates the clutch (shown pulled) and the gearshift by twisting the grip (shown in second position).

It's as simple as that. If you do it as just explained, you'll not have any trouble with this first practice. Keep this point in mind: If you don't give enough power when releasing the clutch in first gear, you'll stall the engine. And if you give too much power, you'll have a jackrabbit start and may lose control of the bike.

Keep another point in mind. It has to do with the *power-to-weight ratio* of the machine under you, and it simply means that any sudden application of power in first (and second) gear will move you forward awfully fast. At this stage of your learning you don't want any surprises of this kind. So practice riding in first gear until you're able to use the clutch and the throttle smoothly and naturally, with the machine under your control.

After riding awhile in first gear, you'll be ready to shift up into second gear, and then into third, and finally into fourth or top gear. Most bikes have a three- or four-speed gearbox; some models have five, six, and even as high as eight gears. The high number of gears does not make shifting complicated. It just means that the machine has a close ratio gearbox designed for smooth acceleration without straining the engine.

Shifting from first to second gear again calls for you to squeeze the clutch, tap the shift lever downward once past the neutral position, then release the clutch and apply power. For second gear the releasing of the clutch does not have to be slow. You can actually let go of the lever and open the throttle the moment you've selected second gear.

Upon reaching second gear, most beginners make the mistake of easing up on the throttle. The physical and emotional tension connected with learning how to handle a live engine causes them to feel that they've accomplished the ultimate by merely reaching second gear, and at this point they expect the engine and the gearbox to take care of things. So they shift into second, let out the clutch, and then dillydally along with the throttle barely open. What happens is that the bike slows down and the engine begins to lug—the thing you don't want the

As bike starts to roll when the clutch is released slowly, rider feeds more gas by twisting right grip. Shifting to next gear calls for pulling the clutch again, shutting off the throttle, selecting the gear with the gear lever, then releasing the clutch as the throttle is opened.

engine to do under any circumstance. So the moment you're in second gear, open the throttle smoothly and get the bike moving. And the same advice holds for the next higher gears.

Keep in mind this rule about shifting: It is better to wind out the engine in a lower gear than to lug it in the wrong high gear.

Only practice in shifting will teach you to recognize the right rpm (revolutions per minute) sound for shifting to the next gear. It's the way experienced riders do it. If your bike is equipped with a tachometer, which tells you how fast the engine is turning, then you may want to use this as a guide for shifting, handling the engine strictly by the book. Many riders use the speedometer as a guide, especially if the face is marked off with numbers to show when to shift to the next gear.

But all it takes is a little practice to recognize the increase or decrease in rpm when you open or close the throttle. Do not race the engine needlessly, and also do not strain it in the wrong gear.

As you're riding around and practicing how to use the clutch and the gears and the brakes, you may experience small difficulties in locating the basic neutral gear position. The reason for the term "basic neutral" position is that many machines have secondary neutrals, usually between next-to-the-top and top gear. Some models, like the M.V. Agusta, have a neutral position between all gears, thus providing the rider with the convenience of a neutral anywhere along the line, and this eliminates the need to shift down three or four times to reach basic neutral.

As soon as you're able to shift from first to second gear, you'll have no trouble shifting through the gears to top gear. Keep up the practice on a straight road, then simulate traffic conditions which call for you to come to a full stop often, and then start up again in first gear.

With right foot against the lowered stand and holding the left handlebar and the frame at the seat, rider can easily lift the machine onto its center stand by pulling back and upward.

Whenever you want to come to a stop during this early practice, always do it by disengaging the clutch and using both the front and the rear brakes. Once stopped, get the gears into neutral. Then start up again in first gear.

After each practice ride, shut off the engine. First pull out the ignition key, or turn it to the off position. And then be sure to close the fuel valve under the tank.

If you shut off the ignition and the engine continues to run, you are faced with the condition known as *preignition*. This means that the inside of the cylinder is coated with carbon deposits which, in their extremely hot state, keep firing off the fuel mixture. To shut off the engine, place the bike in second gear and let out the clutch quickly, stalling the engine. Another way of doing it is to close off the choke. **Preignition** is not desirable, so have the condition remedied.

If you will not be using the bike for a long time, a good technique is to "starve" the engine to a stop. Simply shut off the fuel valve under the tank and let the carb use up all the gas in the line and in the bowl. When the engine dies out, shut off the ignition.

With all this done, lift the machine onto its center stand. This can be done without straining yourself. Roll the machine to where you want to leave it, drop the stand so it touches the ground (be sure the surface is solid), and place the sole of your right foot at the bottom of the stand to keep it from sliding backward. Then turn the handlebar to the left, holding it with your left hand, and with your right hand grab the frame under the seat, or the handle fitted to the frame on some models. Then simply press away with your right foot and at the same time use your arm power to pull upward and to the rear. Try it a few times until it all becomes as easy as lifting a chair.

The outlined practice for handling the clutch and the gears and the brakes is important because it's the only way to prepare yourself for controlling the unexpected situations. Too many beginning riders do not prepare themselves for handling the motorcycle in tight quarters or in slow-moving traffic. All they want to do is open the throttle and roar away at top speed. That kind of riding is too easy, and it's too dangerous.

After a few weeks of practice, you too will find it very easy to speed up through the gears. But the true test still is how well you can handle your bike, under perfect control, at slow speeds, in tight circles, in figure eights, in smooth start-ups, and fast, sure stops.

If you can do all that, your next practice will have to be in shifting down through the gears, because this shifting down is

A rider is maneuvering a Benelli scooter at slow speed, has pulled the clutch, and is ready to shift to next gear.

the mark of the expert. When done correctly, this technique gives you better control of the machine and also saves the wear on brake linings.

For this practice you get up to top gear, let's say fourth, and you begin shifting down. You want to drop back from fourth gear to third gear. Maybe the traffic has slowed, or maybe you've started climbing a hill under insufficient power and speed, and the engine has begun to lug.

Remember this rule for shifting down: Engine rpm must equal the next lower gear's rpm for that road speed. In simpler terms, don't use an idling engine to catch the lower gear. It can be done, all right, but it will wear out the clutch in a hurry.

Using identical H-D Bajas, father and son play tag around an open area of a sandpit.

Dropping one gear lower is not difficult if you remember to keep up the engine rpm after you have selected the next lower gear and just before you let the clutch grab. It works like this: You're doing 40 in top gear (fourth). You pull the clutch (disengage) and lift up the shift lever once for third gear, and you shut the throttle for the instant—but then you open the throttle to rev up the engine, and then you let the clutch grab. Smoothly and without jerking, you have made the shift from fourth to third. Close down the throttle and the bike slows down.

Repeat the same steps, and drop down to second gear, always making sure you rev up the engine before you let the clutch grab.

At this point you have the choice of dropping into neutral or even going into first gear for really slow traveling—or coming to a stop.

Once you get used to the up-through-the-gears and down-through-the-gears game, you'll want to put it to work for practicing circles to the left and right sides. At first your circles may look a little squarish, oval, or otherwise rough. But as you keep running the bike around and around, clutching and shifting, you'll soon develop excellent control.

But don't let the good feeling develop into overconfidence. Overconfidence is like throwing the reins over a horse's neck and letting it take you where it pleases. You want to control the machine all the way and not let it run away from you.

Basic training in handling a motorcycle properly is so important that many major motorcycle companies have sponsored rider training programs for youth groups.

For example, R. D. Rockwood created for Yamaha a complete instructional program which has been used with high school groups to instruct new riders in four basic points: how to start, how to operate, how to stop under normal conditions, and how to stop under emergency conditions. This program points out that speed is not a factor in learning, but perfect control of the machine in first and second gear is. Besides actual practice on lightweight 90-cc Yamaha machines, classroom sessions dealing with written examination requirements of particular states are included in the program.

Similarly, some years ago the Cairo Public School started a pilot training program for the state of Illinois in driver education training for motorcycles, and for this purpose American Jawa provided a dual-control trainer machine—the only machine designed for giving the student actual road-riding practice with the instructor along and in control of the machine in case of emergency.

The makers of the BSA (Birmingham Small Arms) cosponsored, with the Southern California Automobile Club, the Boy Scouts of America, and the Los Angeles Police Department, an instructional program that taught fifteen Boy Scouts how to ride, with the skills and knowledge necessary for safe operation of a motorcycle in today's traffic. The boys were members of Explorer Post 981-X. After classroom work and basic training in riding, the group covered a 200-mile run from La Mirada to Lake Arrowhead Boy Scout Camp over a Saturday and Sunday. The run was supervised, of course, by sponsor personnel, and they did not have so much as a single bad incident.

For interested groups BSA makes available an instructional film, *The Critical Hours*, for classroom use. American Jawa has motocross racing films, and American Honda similarly provides several excellent productions, the most famous of which is *The Invisible Circle* in full color. The mentioned motorcycle companies, along with others, are more than willing to cooperate with authorized leaders of youth groups who want to learn what motorcycling is all about and how to ride safely.

By this time you should be very familiar with the ways of

A California high school group of boys and girls, with their motorcycling instructors and the bikes on which they received their basic riding instruction, which was sponsored and supervised by the police department of their city. (*Yamaha International*)

your own machine. You know, for instance, that anybody can open up a throttle and speed off. But you also know that the big test is not how fast you can run a bike but rather how precisely you can handle it at slow and intermediate speeds.

Can you make it through perfect circles in first and second

Members of Explorer Post 981-X are checked out by instructors before their 200-mile run from La Mirada, California, to Lake Arrowhead camp. (*Birmingham Small Arms*)

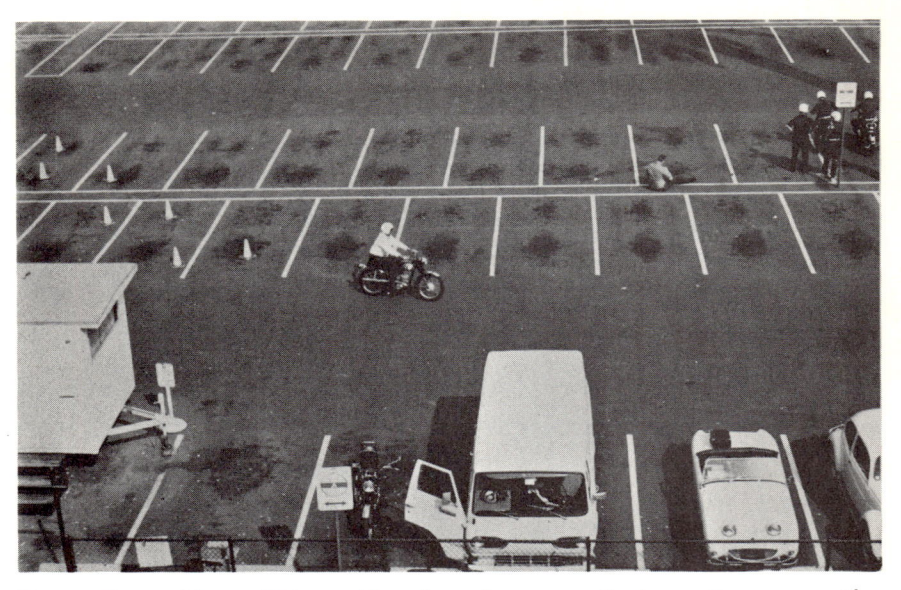

Here a Scout rides a BSA machine through a prescribed practice course. The program covered lectures and riding instruction for safety in traffic long before the run was scheduled. (*Birmingham Small Arms*)

gear and do it to both sides? Can you execute wide and tight figure eights and do it smoothly? Are you able to come to a near stop, nearly standing still, balancing yourself without touching the ground with either foot, and then shift to first gear and move off? Are you able to hold a curve at speed, or do you wobble through it? Do you start off like a jackrabbit because you can't handle the clutch and throttle? How often do you stall the engine? Next time you're out riding, try these maneuvers and see how you make out.

In another chapter you will read about various techniques of skill which you may want to try after you've gained more experience, but at this stage there are two basic techniques you should know. The two techniques have to do with the quick start and the quick, hard stop—both of which can be handy in case of an emergency.

Let's take the quick start first.

For whatever reason, you want to pull away fast from a standstill, and you don't want to mess it up with a stall-out. Don't try a quick start or jackrabbit getaway in tight traffic. Practice on a straight open road where, even if you stall out, you can try again until you get it right. Once you master this technique, you'll find it useful in different situations, including tight traffic.

Your engine is idling, and the gears are in basic neutral. From here on everything will hinge on how well you pour on power and let the clutch grab. Pull the clutch and get into first gear. Now start letting go of the clutch and at the same time open the throttle, winding out the engine. If you make the first ten feet without stalling out, keep going. Then work the clutch, gear lever, and throttle almost together. Pull the clutch as you barely ease off on the power, shift to second, let the clutch pop in, and open up fast. Hit third gear, then fourth. If you do it right, you'll almost slide back off the saddle!

Success depends on not letting up on the power once you decide to go. It's a valuable technique, and it's not difficult even for a beginner.

Now try the fast, hard stop.

This technique may come in handier than the quick start, and you should know how to do it safely. It's very simple: Use both brakes, and use them hard!

What you want is a hard straight-line stop, and you want it under complete control. If you use one brake alone, you have a chance of sliding to one side. Use them together and you'll be surprised how effective they can be.

A warning: If you're in a curve, *do not* use either brake! If you see a curve ahead, use your brakes *before* you reach the curve, or shift down one or two gears, depending on the time you have left in which to do it. You want your machine to be upright when you apply the brakes.

This is one rule you cannot afford to ignore: Don't hit the brakes when you're in a curve.

Heading for Lake Arrowhead, new riders follow the project pace car, entire group maintaining a sensible separation pattern. (*Birmingham Small Arms*)

3 Buying Your First Motorcycle

Before you pick your first motorcycle, decide whether you want a mini, a scooter, a regular street bike, or a hot competition job. By doing this you eliminate a lot of confusion.

Since the minis, scooters, and competition models are rather specialized and do not require complicated comparisons, let's take a look at the great category of regular street bikes. If you know the model or models you like, look in the telephone directory for the nearest dealer. Visit his showroom. Look over the models carefully. Collect all the advertising folders you can, and visit another dealer, where you'll repeat the process.

Visit at least four dealers, and collect material that will help you evaluate the different models. Evaluate them in the quiet of your own room, comparing them feature for feature, item for item, performance for performance, and price for price. This will help you narrow down the field to fewer models over which to worry.

Don't be in a hurry to buy. After you've narrowed it down to two or three machines, talk to riders who own them and see how they feel about their bikes. Ask them how they feel about the particular dealers. Listen carefully. Even then don't be in a hurry. Evaluate what you have read, what you have seen, and what you have heard. For this is the only way in which you can pick the one bike that will be right for you and the one dealer who'll treat you right.

Let's assume that you have decided on a machine. You know the size of the engine in cc's, and you know the weight of this machine. You're sure you want to buy this model because it has all the features you like. It looks good, and you hope it will handle nicely when you get your demonstration ride.

This is the time to check out the bike with your family's insurance broker. The reason the insurance broker enters the picture is that most states require you to carry basic property damage and personal liability insurance. This is where the weight of the motorcycle and the size of the engine become important in certain states, because insurance rates are often computed on this basis. Rates vary of course from state to state and even from locality to locality in the same state. In New York, for example, the rate for an under-300-pound machine (called a lightweight) is nearly half that of anything over 300 pounds.

Right at the start you'll be faced with insurance costs. If you plan to use the machine for relaxed tooling around in town, the all-around costs of owning a lightweight will pay off in many ways. If you want better performance because you'll be climbing steep grades and sometimes carrying a friend as a passenger, and money is not a problem, then you'll need a machine with a bigger engine. This would be the place to compare the available models with the same size engines to see if perhaps one of them is under 300 pounds, or whatever weight requirements will keep you in the lower-cost insurance bracket.

When you buy a new machine, be sure you understand the terms of the warranty. Have the salesman explain the fine print. Be sure that an owner's manual, and if possible a parts catalog, is given to you, along with a set of tools. Many riders also purchase a shop manual in which they can find detailed

When selecting a two-wheeler, check the ground to seat-top distance. Rider's feet should comfortably reach the ground.

Sitting on the motorcycle, the rider must feel right when he holds the handlebars. Clutch and brake levers must be within easy reach—fingers, hand, and wrist forming a straight line.

repair and overhaul procedures, just in case they want to tinker with their motorcycle.

Before you make your final decision, get the salesman to take you for a demonstration ride. But remember that this kind of riding has nothing to do with how the bike will feel when you take over the handlebars. What you learn from a demonstration ride is the feel of power or the lack of it as the machine is taken through the gears. If you pay attention, you'll also find out whether or not the engine is easy or hard to start. And if you go over rough roads, you'll learn how good the suspension is.

When you return to the showroom, do what experienced riders do when they begin evaluating a new machine.

First, remember that sitting on a stationary bike may feel very comfortable. But you must also feel comfortable once the bike is under way and going over different kinds of road surfaces. Comfort and handling go together. You must feel at ease in the saddle, and once under way, the bike must handle easily and naturally. There are models that look as if they can outperform anything on the street, then turn out to be unstable and hard-riding.

Second, make sure your feet reach the ground easily when the bike is off the center stand. This is an important point, because a high seat can be awkward in stop-and-go traffic. Another thing about the seat or saddle is its width, which can be uncomfortable if too narrow or if too wide.

Third, do the handlebars feel too narrow or too wide? While they can be adjusted for height, they cannot be squeezed or forced apart. In connection with handlebars, remember that the extremely high type, called ape-hangers, not only are illegal in most states but do not give you good control of the machine.

Fourth, look down and see where the exhaust pipe is in relation to your leg, and then decide whether or not this may be awkward once the pipe gets hot. Yes, the special shielding around the pipe will protect you, but a hot pipe and very warm shield in hot weather can be a nuisance. If not a nuisance for you, it may be one for your passenger.

Fifth, check the hand controls and the foot controls to see whether they work easily. Are the foot-operated levers spaced sensibly when you try to shift or use the brake pedal? Also check the swing of the kick starter to see if your toe or heel catches in the peg.

Sixth, if the salesman starts up the engine, note whether it fired on the first or second kick or if starting was difficult. And once the engine is running, decide if the exhaust sound is the kind you can live with.

Seventh, sound the horn. It should be clear and loud, not feeble like a weak buzzer. It's also a good idea to check the brightness of the headlight and the effectiveness of the stoplight at the rear.

The next step is for you to ride the machine yourself. Ask the salesman to let you take the machine for a trial run.

Start up the engine—yourself. Decide whether it was easy or hard. Next, make up your mind not to abuse the machine in any way. Take the bike out for a ride, go up and down through the gears, handle the brakes, and do the whole thing over and over.

What you want to find out is how the bike behaves in your hands. Everybody handles a bike differently. You handle it your way. You are now the test rider putting the machine through its paces, checking if the handling and comfort suit you. Now you'll find out if the suspension system reacts well on a rough road, if the engine pulls effortlessly when you open up, if the brakes are tops or just so-so, if the bike wobbles or runs straight after hitting a bump, and if the overall riding qualities are comfortable or leave something to be desired.

Learn about these things *before* you sign the purchase order.

Now that you own a motorcycle, you'll need certain basic equipment to go with it, and this equipment has to do with both safety and comfort.

Make sure you have at least one mirror (on the left handlebar); another mirror on the right handlebar gives you an even better view of what's behind you. But don't neglect to turn your head to make doubly sure what's behind you before you change lanes or start a turn.

If you read even one copy of any motorcycling magazine, you'll learn about the pros and cons of wearing a helmet. In many states the law says motorcycle riders must wear a helmet and must also wear shatterproof eye protection, usually in the form of goggles or a face shield. Anyone who has ever taken a spill on a motorcycle will vouch for the benefits of helmet and goggles, especially if his head hits the road, a wall, a tree, or the side of a car. Since competition riders wear both, there is no possible reason for not wearing a helmet and eye protection.

Competition riders wear special boots and padded gloves to protect their hands and feet in case of a spill. They don't expect to spill any more than you do, but they wear these items, along with heavy trousers and jackets, just in case. So make it a rule to wear full shoes (no sandals and certainly no barefoot riding!) and gloves to suit the weather conditions. For wintertime riding you'll need heavy, lined clothing, and for the rainy season you'll need special waterproof coveralls.

With your equipment and machine ready to ride, you're still faced with two legal requirements: Your machine must be registered with the State Department of Motor Vehicles and must carry a license tag, and you must be licensed to operate your machine. Normally the dealer is willing to help you on both counts.

Many states issue a junior motorcycle operator's permit or license for fifteen- and sixteen-year-old riders.

The riding test itself is never so difficult that a rider who knows how to handle a machine cannot pass the first time out. The details of the written test and riding test will be covered in the next chapter.

4 Riding in Traffic

The laws for registering a motorcycle and licensing a driver vary from state to state. Visit your local Department of Motor Vehicles and ask for all the booklets available for motorcycle riders. This is your only way of familiarizing yourself with what you must know and how your bike must be equipped.

Here are a few examples from the New York State manual:

1. Riders are not allowed to ride more than two motorcycles abreast in any one traffic lane.
2. You are not allowed to ride a motorcycle between rows of cars in lanes of traffic or between lane traffic cars and those parked at the curb or at the side of the road.
3. You are not allowed to pass other vehicles on the edge of the lane. (In order to pass a car you must move into the adjoining lane.)
4. You must use hand signals (or lights, if your machine is equipped with them) to indicate your intention to stop or to make a turn. (For stopping, extend your left arm downward at your hip with palm facing to the rear; for a left turn hold your left arm straight out to the left at shoulder level; for a right turn crook your left arm at the elbow so that your hand is pointing over your head to the right.)
5. Day or night, you must ride with your lights on.

The state manuals or booklets will give you a good deal of other valuable information that will help you pass your written and riding tests. For example, you'll learn which special roads or parkways are closed to you, how you're expected to park your bike in city streets, and that certain bridges may be closed to you on very windy days.

The inspector who conducts your road test will want you to demonstrate how well you can handle a motorcycle and how familiar you are with traffic rules. With sufficient practice on your part the riding test should be easy.

You'll be asked to run your bike in circles within a small square area and then in figure eights in a larger area. You may be asked to ride in traffic to show how well you can handle the bike on the road, while the inspector follows in a car. In some instances you may have to demonstrate a zigzag run between rubber cones.

Generally, the test is easy, but what can make it difficult is your nervousness, physical tension, or the desire to drive perfectly. Now think back to your practice (in isolated areas away from traffic, if you didn't have a rider's permit, or on the roads and in the streets with a licensed rider along, if you had a permit). All that practice was meant to give you the confidence and the know-how for the riding test. Imagine your inspector is another enthusiast (which he probably is) and that you're showing him how well you can do things on two wheels. Relax and ride your bike as if it's the only thing you've ever done.

Now that you have a driver's license and your bike has a registration tag, you can ride in traffic. This calls for concentration and patience. You must keep in lane and flow with the rest of the motorists, speeding up or slowing down as the traffic demands. You must be aware of every car near you; you must anticipate situations that may develop twenty cars ahead. A motorcyclist must always be prepared for the unexpected.

To better understand your position in traffic, imagine that you are an automobile driver following a motorcycle. You're driving alone on a four-lane highway. You're in the fast lane with the slower traffic on your right. There is a motorcycle driver in front of you traveling at 10 miles below the speed limit. Now all that you want is for the rider to either increase his speed to what the limit permits or move to the right into the slower lane so that you can pass him.

You blip your horn once. There's plenty of room in the right lane. You know he heard your horn. But he continues to ride in front of you. So you blow your horn again. The motorcycle rider doesn't even turn his head. So you pass him on the right side. He looks at you, and you give him a look of anger. And then you decide that all motorcycle riders are arrogant fools and should not be permitted on the roads.

Put yourself in another example. You're sitting at the wheel of your car in the middle of a city street, waiting for the light to turn green. A motorcycle rider is alongside you, and he too is waiting for the light to turn green. Then, as soon as the light turns green, both of you move ahead in the normal manner, except that the rider speeds up a little more and then cuts in front of your car—and turns into the avenue. His turn forces you to jam on your brakes, and you again decide that motorcycle riders as a lot are not very smart.

For the next example of how *not* to act in traffic, you are again behind the wheel of your car, and you're barely moving, bumper to bumper. All the cars are tightly lined up in lanes, and suddenly a motorcycle roars through between the cars, just missing doors and fenders. You growl and shake your head in disbelief. What would happen to the bike rider if one of the cars suddenly moved into his path? Well, again you decide that all motorcycle riders are arrogant fools and should not be permitted on the roads.

69

You can help the sport of motorcycling by making a good impression with sensible, skillful driving. In traffic hundreds of people will instantly witness your attitude all within a mere fifty-mile range of riding. It's the big test.

Now let's discuss the actual traffic riding techniques that you need in order to ride in utmost safety. The techniques revolve around conditions, and these can be sorted out as follows:

Separation.
Speed.
Quick Start—Panic Stop.
Passing.
Horn Signals.
Headlight—Rear Lights.
Rain.
Intersections.
Distractions.

As you know, aircraft are separated from each other in flight by air traffic controllers in airport towers. Separation provides safety for every plane. As a motorcycle rider you must see to it that you have plenty of separation in the road traffic that surrounds you. You must be your own traffic controller.

Whenever you ride close behind another car, you are ignoring the factor of safety that *separation* provides. If the car in front of you stops suddenly, for any reason whatever, you'll need enough separation in which to react—either for stopping or for moving into the next lane. Stopping at slow speed is not a problem, but tailgating the end of a car at 50 or 60 is stupid.

The higher your speed, the greater should be your separation. At high speed everything becomes more critical—your reaction time, road surface conditions, brake effectiveness. Also bear in mind that at high speed any distraction—looking too long at the scenery, watching another car or motorcycle, talking over your shoulder to your passenger—can suddenly reduce your separation to the danger point. Keep your mind on separation! If you must look at something, make it a glance. If you must tell your passenger something, keep your eyes front. If you want to look at the scenery, pull off the road and enjoy the view.

A road-safety slogan says "Speed kills," but the experts tell us that speed in the right place and under the right conditions does not kill. What kills is the wrong rider speeding in the wrong place.

Most motorcycles are lightweight machines with excellent power-to-weight ratios, which means they can pick up speed fast. They can also stop fast. So too many riders get the idea that they can control this easily. They can, under the right conditions. But under the wrong conditions—speeding and then having the unexpected suddenly loom up—they meet with disaster.

You can learn a great deal by watching how the experts handle their machines in street traffic. Their technique is in the correct use of the gearbox. They start up smoothly, flow with the traffic, maintaining speed and also maintaining separation, and they ease to smooth, controlled stops every time. They almost never resort to jackrabbit starts. They don't wind out the engine to the red line in every gear; they don't weave in and out of lanes or between tightly packed cars. And so they never slam into such obstructions as trees, curbs, rear ends or sides of cars, trucks, or buses.

Now, let's take a look at passing. Whenever you pass another vehicle, obey the rules of the road, always signaling your intention and always being on the alert so as not to be surprised by another vehicle. The whole secret for successful passing is in the word "surprise": You don't want to surprise the driver behind you and certainly not the driver of the car you're passing.

Never pass if you cannot see what's ahead.

Never squeeze into a position between cars in order to pass.

And always glance back before you start passing! Even if your mirror doesn't show anything bearing down on you, glance back to make sure that the mirror isn't lying.

If you have directional light signals on your motorcycle, use them to show the driver behind you what you intend to do; or use hand signals, as required by law.

The use of the horn by motorcycle riders is a touchy subject. Some say you should use it to let car drivers know you're near them, and others say you should ride in such a manner that the use of the horn is completely unnecessary.

Most motorcycle horns produce a high-pitched sound, and most car drivers don't like to hear that high-pitched sound, particularly if it's close at their side. It has a startling effect, even an irritating one. Use the horn as a signal only.

The headlight and rear lights of your machine should be in perfect working order whenever you ride at night. Before starting out, check the operation of your low and high beams and the rear stoplight. If the glass of either lamp is dirty, wipe it clean so that it gives best illumination and that others may easily see you.

When you ride at night, you should be twice as cautious as when you ride in daytime. Keep in mind that various light reflections may confuse you, and any momentary confusion can spell trouble. Fast riding compounds your problems. And wearing sunglasses at night is about as necessary as pointing your exhaust pipes to the front.

All vehicles behave one way on a dry surface and an entirely different way on a wet surface. When a car skids on four wheels, it's nothing more than a skid. But when a two-wheeler skids on a wet surface, it's usually a bad spill, with damage to the machine and the rider.

A motorcycle rider in traffic always signals his intentions. Note stoplight overhead and signal that bike will be brought to a stop.

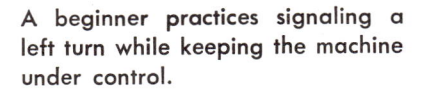

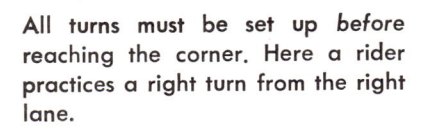

A beginner practices signaling a left turn while keeping the machine under control.

All turns must be set up *before* reaching the corner. Here a rider practices a right turn from the right lane.

If you're riding and it begins to rain, remember that this beginning rain and the oil and dirt on the road will form a very slippery substance. If the rain continues to fall in a downpour, the water will wash away the oil and dirt, so you'll be able to ride at higher speeds (not meaning wide open). Needless to say, you'll be wearing effective rain gear.

If you add the darkness of night to the rain, you have the most critical riding condition. At night the wetness reflects every light source, even when that light source is far from you. These reflections have a way of confusing you, and they also have a way of confusing car drivers. For this reason experienced motorcycle riders avoid the combination of night and rain.

Did you know that most accidents take place at intersections? Wherever one road crosses another or feeds into it, there is the possibility that somebody isn't going to pay attention to the STOP or YIELD sign or to the control light. So you as a motorcycle rider need only one piece of advice as you approach an intersection. *Do not* depend on the signs or on the control light. Look to all sides as you slow down, and then either ride through or make your turn. And whenever you make any turn, always make it from the proper lane so that you don't cut in front of a car.

While the car is the main thing on the road that you must be concerned with, aside from weather conditions which make riding dangerous, there will be a few surprises waiting for you nevertheless.

The worst is the iron-grated bridge surface, or trolley tracks, maybe even railroad tracks. Riding a motorcycle parallel to any track or to a deep cut in the road surface can easily cause loss of control. As you ride along, you won't be aware that you're approaching these hazards, and they'll take you by surprise. About the only defense you have is to watch far enough ahead in order to spot these hazards. On iron-grated bridges, slow down; if possible, cross the bridge at an angle—even a slight angle helps. As for tracks and deep cuts in the road, cross them at sharp angles, always.

Now consider man's best friend, the dog. For some reason even the friendliest dog seems to like to chase motorcycles. You'll be riding along a street or a lonely road, and all of a sudden you'll hear a rushing sound behind you and then the outburst of barking. Yes, you'll be scared. Being scared is natural, depending on the size of the dog, but don't let yourself fly into a panic. Riders report that a barking dog will keep a distance as he continues to run slightly behind you and to the side, all the while barking. They claim he's bluffing, and that he will not come closer. Some riders report that when they come to a stop the dog comes to a halt too and continues barking. But everything depends on the disposition of the dog, so advice is risky here. You can easily outdistance him, but in heavy traffic this too is risky—either you or the dog can get hurt. On an open road the advice is to keep pouring it on and get rid of the nuisance.

As a dog is attracted to motorcycle riders, so is a bee. This problem arises when you wear loose-fitting clothing—the bee accidentally flies inside your shirt, you become aware of your problem and start a wild brushing away with one or both hands trying to get to the bee, and this leaves the bike free to run into an accident. Advice: Don't wear loose clothing. A bee also has a way of flying in under a face shield, in which case simply lift up the shield and let the rush of air take care of the bee.

So far most of your riding has been solo. Riding in pairs or in large groups calls for more caution on the part of every rider and also for prearranged signals to be used to let everyone know what to do in traffic.

A group of riders keeps in line and not too close together. The leader sets a sensible pace.

If you and a friend are riding on a wide open road, the side-by-side method is all right. If traffic is heavy, then one bike should follow the other, with adequate separation.

If you take the lead, glance back often to see if your friend is still with you. Any number of minor reasons could cause him to stop, and at speed it's not likely that you'll hear his horn signal. Also, pace yourself in traffic so that you don't create tight or dangerous situations for him. Don't speed through a light that has just turned amber. The lead rider, whether for two machines or a club of twenty, must think for the riders behind him as well as for himself.

There are three conditions that take the fun out of riding: an accident, an engine that won't start, and a flat tire.

By this time you know how to handle yourself in traffic so as not to have an accident.

You'll be told how to troubleshoot an ailing engine in another chapter.

That leaves a flat tire, the curse of all riders whether in city traffic, on the highway, or in competition.

When it happens to you—and it will, sooner or later—you can have it repaired if you're near a gas station where the mechanic is willing to do the job. Or you can do it yourself. Since it's not an impossible task, let's see how you go about it.

First, when you buy your bike, check the tool kit to make sure it contains tire irons. Some manufacturers include them, some don't. Then read the owner's manual to see how the manufacturer wants you to handle the wheel, tire, and tube. Even if the tool kit includes tire irons, it is not likely to contain a tube repair kit of scraper, patches, and glue, or a tire pump (Jawa models feature a pump). So you'll have to buy these items for the inevitable emergency.

The easiest way to patch a tube is to get the wheel off the machine, unscrew the valve from the stem, and let all the air out of the tube (walk around on the edge of the tire, with the wheel flat on the ground). Then pry one side of the tire off the rim. For the prying job, use a tire iron—not a screwdriver!

If a nail caused your trouble, you might be able to find the nail in the tire and so locate the hole in the tube. Otherwise you'll have to inflate the tube partially and then locate the spot where air is escaping. If you're near a creek, simply dunk the tube and watch for telltale bubbles.

Once you have located the hole, rub it down with the scraper. If you don't have a scraper, use a rough file. Usually the tube repair kit gives you the simple steps for patching— apply the glue to the tube, then peel the backing off the patch and fit the patch in place. You do all this, of course, with all the air let out of the tube.

Then you must fit the tube back into the tire carefully, then fit the tire onto the rim, without pinching the tube and causing another puncture. Be sure to center the valve stem through the rim hole, then begin fitting the tire into place. After you've completed the whole job, check the tire around the rim to make sure it is correctly seated, screw in the valve, then use the hand pump to inflate the tube to the correct pressure.

This is not an easy or enjoyable job, so check your tires for imbedded nails after every run.

5 Techniques and Skill

The motorcycle, like the human body, has limitations. You can jump only so far. You can lift only so much. You can stay underwater only so long. When you're tired, your mind and body slow down. These are your limitations.

The motorcycle can go only so fast, can stop only so quickly, and can take only so much stress. These are the limits of its performance, and it means that you can't make a street bike do things that a true competition machine is able to do.

If you are planning to practice rough riding at a sandpit or a scramble course, be sure you have the machine that can take the abuse.

And even if you're riding the right bike, after a day of hard riding practice be sure to clean up the machine. Sand and dirt have a way of packing in around the chain, sprockets, and other parts of the engine, wheels, and frame.

When you see an experienced motorcycle rider snap the front wheel of his bike off the ground and keep it up for a long run, you'll be tempted to try it too. If you happen to watch the riders in a motocross spin their machines around the hairpin turns, you too will want to get out there and try it. If you try these things and succeed, all will be well and good. But if you spill and if you hurt yourself, you won't like it.

The way to learn how to ride like the experts is to take it

Miroslav Halm, famous competitor from Czechoslovakia, tears uphill on a CZ to win the heat at Unadilla, New York, in 1970.

one step at a time. Take each step slowly enough to make sure you can handle it. The experts didn't just up and do it. They learned their techniques in easy steps.

What you're really about to learn is how to handle your bike under harder conditions than those of city and road riding. You'll be practicing at a sandpit or some other area where this kind of riding is allowed. Right from the start, keep in mind that you'll use caution throughout. You want to learn, not damage your bike and yourself.

First, inspect every important part of your machine, including the tires and the chain. Make sure all bolts are tight.

Then start up the engine and slowly ride around the area where you intend to practice, and check out the location of rocks, ruts, mounds, logs, mud puddles, old tires left lying around, and anything else that looks like an obstruction. And, finally, stake out your own area where you'll begin your first practice at becoming a hard rider.

Knowing how to *swerve* a machine suddenly can often mean the difference between a crash and getting out of a tight spot alive. Swerving means to change directions suddenly and at the risk of having the bike slide out from under you, which is also called "laying her down."

Imagine yourself riding behind a car in traffic, and the car comes to a sudden stop, so sudden in fact that you are totally unprepared to brake to a full stop. You don't want to slam wheel first into the car, so, to avoid a crash, you swerve sideways. Even if you hit the car this way, you're better off than going in headfirst. (Remember the rule about riding with separation? Had you maintained separation, you wouldn't be faced with this problem.)

To practice swerving, select a fairly hard surface at a sandpit and approach it at about 20 miles per hour. Keep your body relaxed. Hold the handlebars lightly, letting your elbows and

At moderate speed, the rider swings his 350-cc Jawa from a right to a left curve by simply leaning into it. Too much lean lays the bike down.

With left foot acting as the pivot, the rider leans the bike over hard and guns it around to the left. Note right foot near the brake pedal.

The lean and slide of the rear wheel keep the machine spinning around. If control is lost, pull clutch and shut the throttle.

shoulders absorb the shocks. As you approach the spot where you intend to swerve, wiggle your buttocks on the seat to get even more of a feel of the bike under you. Plan the swerve to the right.

Using your hips and buttocks, gently push leftward against the seat, and at the same time very lightly press the right handlebar *forward*—very lightly!

The moment you press the right handlebar forward, you'll feel the machine lean to the right. If you keep up the pressure, you'll be going into a right-side swerve.

Straighten out, circle back to your starting point, and go through the same maneuver again—but this time do it a bit more quickly. Sharpen the swerve. Then straighten out. Then with your hips and buttocks push the seat toward the right side, and with your left hand push against the left handlebar. Swerve to the left. Straighten out.

If you press too much, you'll slide the bike out. Your hand pressure against the handlebar shouldn't be too hard. A kind of quick jab, coupled with the right lean, does it nicely. At first you may doubt that a motorcycle will go to the right when the right handlebar is pressed *away* from the curve line. But if you do it the way it was explained, you'll find that it works and that it's exciting.

Whether you're on dirt or on concrete or macadam, overcontrol can result in a spill. And you can be sure of a spill if you try it on a wet or oily surface.

While practicing swerves and even laying the bike down, try to develop a feel for the machine's reaction to your hand and body movements. Keep relaxed. When the bike starts to slide out from under you, have the presence of mind to slide your foot along the ground on the lean side. You don't want the bike to trap your foot underneath.

If you happen to be watching an expert doing fast swerves

from side to side, note the way he keeps his head upright in relation to the ground. This trick gives the rider a better perspective and feel of the machine.

At the sandpits a quick turning around in one spot comes in as a practical maneuver when you suddenly decide that you want to go back from where you came. Some call it a *spin-around*.

All that you have to do is lean the machine hard over to one side, low gear selected and the clutch pulled, then play the clutch and the throttle so that the rear wheel spins—but without grabbing the ground too solidly. If the rear wheel bites into the ground too hard, the machine may run away from you.

The whole trick is to balance yourself and the bike on your supporting foot, which acts as the center of the circle. By keeping the handlebar turned slightly into the turn, the bike will go around and around so long as you play the clutch and the throttle right.

If the machine starts to run away from you, simply shut the throttle and pull the clutch.

To carry this spin-around to its logical conclusion, after you've spun the bike around once or twice, straighten out the handlebar, snap the bike upright, and then ride off in a straight line—just the way motocross racers do.

More likely than not, the sandpit will have some fairly steep dirt hills, and you'll surely want to run your machine up and down these grades. Remember that it's easier running a hill if the ground is hard; if it's soft ground, you can easily bog down right in the middle of it.

Let's try it *downhill* first. You'll find it easy, because all you have to do is keep your body weight farther back on the seat —or over it, if you're standing up on the pegs. In this way you'll have better control of the bike once you start heading

Rider keeps his body weight to the rear when running downhill. In unfamiliar areas it is dangerous to run downhill too fast.

When running uphill, rider leans forward and usually keeps off the seat. Power usually must be on all the way.

down. When you reach the bottom of the hill, take your natural sitting position.

On a long downhill run, don't overdo it with a lot of speed. Keep power on, but only enough to give you good control. Keep your eyes ahead, searching for rocks, tree branches, ruts, and anything that may be in your way to cause a problem. And if you must use the brakes, don't slam them on.

For an *uphill* run, select a short slope, and make sure no rider will be coming your way once you start up. Keep to a low gear, and keep the power on. As you approach the hill and start up, lean your body forward over the tank—and stay there. Keep power on all the way.

When you reach the top of the hill, ease off on the power and take your natural position on the seat. If you come up too fast, you'll find your bike leaving the ground in a jump. This

At high speed this motocross racer takes a hill in good form during practice. Note position of body off the seat.

is not serious under the circumstances or unusual. Just remember two things about running up a hill: You need power all the way, and that same power may produce a jump at the top of the hill.

It's the hill that dictates the amount of power and the gear to use.

If anything goes wrong halfway up and you find yourself bogging down, don't try to hold the bike upright with your legs. Simply lean to one side and fall over, and if possible keep the clutch pulled until you can kill the engine. Some machines have a kill-button on the handlebar for this exact purpose—by pressing the kill-button the rider shorts out the ignition to stall the engine.

Jumping a motorcycle is common practice by riders in *enduro* or *motocross* races. Racing against time, these riders don't slow down when they approach low or high mounds, or when they go into a gully or tear uphill out of one. They just ride at the highest speed possible under the conditions.

For the average rider, jumping a motorcycle is simply a stunt, and the worst of it is that the stunt abuses many of the mechanical parts of the machine. The average bike designed for street and road riding can't take too many jumps and not show the signs of the strain.

So let's assume that you have the right machine. Play it smart. For your first jumps, find a small mound at the sandpit. Approach the mound from a distance that will let you get into second gear. The size of your jump will depend on the speed with which you go over the mound and how you carry your body once the wheels leave the ground.

Using the same technique as when you ran uphill, lean slightly forward and keep power on. Not too fast. As you go up the mound, lean back, extend your arms, and lift yourself off the seat onto the pegs.

This young rider controls his jumping bike perfectly as he reaches the top of the hill—with power still on.

Once the bike leaves the ground during a jump, the rider must correctly manage his body in order to keep things in control. Here the machine is about to settle on its rear wheel, as it should.

Once airborne, keep the handlebars straight and steady—in line with your path. Since your first jump is rather small and short, you might come down on both wheels at the same time. If you do, you're doing well. If you come down on the rear wheel first, that's even better.

But *never* come down on the front wheel first!

Don't become overconfident.

Bigger and longer jumps, using the right machines, are only a matter of experience, the development of an instinctive feel for jumping.

The sandpit is a good place to find out how fast you can bring your bike from speed to a full stop. On level ground, it's no problem at all. Just get on the brakes together, and there's your hard stop.

But suppose you're running over rutted ground, parallel to the ruts? Motocross riders find that they must use the brakes under such conditions and do it without losing control. They approach a curve which has several grooves dug through it by the wheel of every machine that had gone through, and each rider plays the power and the brakes to get around as fast as he can, without spilling. How do they do it?

What may appear to be a bold use of brakes in a curve is in reality the only right way to use the brakes—the wheels must be vertical to whatever the surface. In a slow-motion projection of the motorcycle speeding through a curve and the rider using the brakes, you notice that the wheels are in contact with the ground at a right angle, or nearly so. Doing it any other way would send the bike and rider into a spill.

You can experiment with this technique in easy stages. Running slowly, head into a lazy curve and then apply the front brake, and see what happens. The rear wheel will come around, and if you have too much speed, you'll fall. Make another slow run, and this time apply only the rear brake as

Approaching a mound for jumping practice, rider keeps power on and pulls up on the handlebars.

As both wheels leave the ground, rider keeps the front wheel straight and leans slightly backward.

you enter a curve. The bike will either snap upright or go out from under you.

Convince yourself how easy it is to spill if you use the brakes improperly, and then bear in mind the rule to *keep your bike upright whenever you brake hard.*

The spectacular technique of riding a motorcycle with the front wheel off the ground involves considerable coordination between throttle, clutch, and weight distribution of the rider. Many race riders, after getting the winner's flag, will *wheelie* along in front of the grandstand and do it for great distances with perfect control.

Some machines, because of power and gearing, are easy to snap into a wheelie. Other bikes just haven't the right setup in this department.

You can find out quickly enough if your bike has the ability

Bike should be landed on the rear wheel, and rider should be off the seat. Note deflection of rear tire.

to wheelie. Find a hard surface at the sandpit, then engage first gear and hold the clutch. Open the throttle for some power, and then let the clutch grab fast and hard. If the bike has it, you'll surge forward and you'll feel the front wheel lifting up. But by instinct you'll shut the throttle and slow down.

Now try it again, but this time, when the bike starts to move forward, pour on more power and lean slightly back on the seat. As the front wheel comes up, try running a short distance, lean forward, and then ease off on the power. Make several runs this way until you develop a feel for the bike and its ability (or lack of ability) to bring the front wheel up.

Machines with very low gearing can be wheelied quite easily. As a matter of fact, some of them literally leap into the air, standing almost vertically on the rear wheel, and the rider is thus forced to dismount. Therefore, if anything goes wrong with your attempts to wheelie, simply cut the power and pull the clutch.

Developing the described techniques of skill is a challenge, of course, and once learned can be quite enjoyable. However a new rider should always remember that all techniques are best learned when done in easy stages.

Let's suppose you have a friend who wants to go riding with you but who has never before been on the back seat of a motorcycle. The first two-up advice is for you to explain to your friend what to expect and how to ride with you.

For example, explain to your friend to sit upright and forward and not to lean in the opposite direction when you go into a curve. Also, not to clown once you get under way. Your friend can be a real help in signaling your intentions to stop or turn. Make sure your passenger is wearing full shoes, gloves, helmet, and eye shield. Ten minutes of an explanation is not a long time, but one spill can put a would-be motorcycling enthusiast off the sport forever.

Another way in which motorcycling enthusiasts enjoy their bikes is by riding the trails through the woods and across open country, where such trails are open to the sport. Since the sport has been developing fast, manufacturers have been designing special machines for this kind of off-the-road riding.

Many trail machines are completely equipped so that they can be licensed for road use as well, while for trail riding they are outfitted with spark arresters in the exhaust system to eliminate the possibility of igniting dry grass and causing fires.

Trail-riding techniques call for a little more caution because you'll be riding across unfamiliar territory. Riding the trails is for enjoyment, not for racing through the woods and underbrush at top speed. You're out to enjoy nature, by yourself or with a group, and you want to make the right impression on everyone who may meet you along the trail.

Here are a few pointers:

Give pedestrians the right-of-way—and smile at them. Avoid streets and residential areas as much as possible. Before you leave your base of operations, let someone know which way you're headed. And no matter where you park your machine, be sure to shut off the fuel valve and remove the ignition key.

While riding, keep your hands on the grips and your feet on the pegs, and if there had been any rain and the ground appears soft, be doubly careful. If you lose control on a hill and fall over, get off the machine on the uphill side. If the engine stalls while you're climbing a hill, use the front brake to hold the bike in place, and again dismount on the uphill side.

Motorcycle racing is a subject unto itself. It can be further divided into such special events as short dirt track racing, straight scramble, a very long road race, a closed-circuit motocross, a cross-country endurance race, and any one of many other kinds of races. Each kind of race has its followers of course, but somehow two of the most popular in the United States are the motocross and the enduro, while in Europe the long road race seems to have more appeal.

To get a closer view of a long road race, we interviewed Joseph Rottigni, who at one time had raced in Italy and had also competed in the International Six Day Trials (ISDT) in Germany (1956) and in Czechoslovakia (1957). In Joe's words:

"I started the way I suppose many young fellows start—I worked after school in a machine shop, and next to the shop was a motorcycle shop, so all day long I heard the sound of

Roaring toward the finish line at Unadilla during the 1970 Motocross, Miroslav Halm takes the jumps easily. . . .

Then, passing the flagman, Halm wheelies his CZ in perfect control past the cheering spectators.

engines. You might say this is what attracted me in the first place. I played soccer in Bergamo for about a year and a half, but every year a road race was held in Bergamo's old town. . . . Bergamo is seven hundred years old, built on a hill, with narrow streets and sharp turns, and so we kids used to watch the race.

"Well, the race got us, so every lunch hour about thirty of us would race . . . sure, the police tried to stop us, but we raced every time we could. Later on I worked for the Parilla motorcycle factory, and I became very familiar with this machine. I actually started in endurance (enduro) racing and then went to road racing. Twelve years ago it was different, the European style was for the rider to keep his feet on the pegs and his body low. About four or five years ago this style started becoming popular in the United States, too. Our usual road race was anywhere from 50 to 75 kilometers, and the endurance runs were about 350 kilometers. I enjoyed the enduro because it's a tough race, through woods, water, mud, sand, everything.

"The Six Day Trials is different again. You have twenty-nine nations competing, and you may have three hundred riders starting . . . not many finish, of course . . . my own Parilla broke down . . . that year the Czechs won the race. You must have a good machine to win any race, and then comes mental and physical preparation . . . you must be prepared for the race.

"Like other riders, I owned my machine and I had to service it myself. You race because you like to race . . . just like others like to climb mountains. The biggest race I won was the Giro D'Italia, the nine-day race around Italy. It's a race against time, four riders starting out every thirty seconds. The weather was mostly rain and snow. My Parilla was a Formula 3 machine, capable of 150 kilometers per hour. The first day we covered 175 kilometers, then averaged about 220. The longest run was 378. In that race were such riders as Venturi,

Libanori, Zubani, Tartarini. Some of the racers hit speeds of 200 per hour! I guess I liked road racing because you could achieve such high speeds, but then one mistake can cost you the race. Also don't forget that twelve years ago you couldn't do what's possible today—if you start comparing speeds—because today you have improved designs in machines, and specially in tires.

"Like in everything else, there are techniques. You keep your eyes on the tachometer. You must be aware of what the machine is doing . . . the carburetor, ignition, gears, clutch. When you realize that a 50-cc engine with seven or twelve gears is good for 100 miles per hour, you also realize that you must not miss a shift point. If you miss a shift, you're in trouble. Much of it is a matter of experience . . . it's up to the rider. One day you know you can do it, and another day you know you can't. When the competition is tight, for example, you've got to know to hold back and to make your move carefully. If you go too fast, speed will exceed traction and you'll have a drift. You must control it. If you can't, you have trouble. You sense these things, you feel them. My own technique was to fit my body to the circumstances, switching weight, leaning, pulling the bike . . . it was right for me, maybe not good for somebody else.

"What advice would I give? Well, not to become overconfident. And to keep the machine in good shape. If you let the machine go, it becomes more expensive in the long run."

Participating in fifteen races in one season running from May to October, James Cooke placed third several times in three-quarter-mile speed track events, scrambles, and motocross races, all of them taking place in Japan and mostly against Japanese riders. In Jim's words:

"Yes, there are some differences in racing in Japan. Here in

This young rider kept this wheelie going quite a distance. To stop a runaway wheelie, shut the power off or hit the rear brake. Note position of rider's feet, just in case.

Lifting a 90-cc Jawa Trail bike into a wheelie is easy, but too much power can cause a complete rollover.

Rider on this Benelli 200-cc Sprite shifts his weight, pours it on, and lifts up the front wheel for some fun riding.

Two-up on a H-D heavyweight in full dress. The young rider is actually in control of a 900-pound machine, with father along to help a little when they come to a stop.

Down the path and up the hill on a 90-cc Jawa Trail bike provide this rider with a thrilling and satisfying sport.

A group of trail riders and their bikes alongside a lake. Trail riding should be done only on designated paths.

For long cross-country touring, many riders prefer a heavier and more powerful machine—like a 650-cc Benelli shown in this scenic view. (Cosmopolitan Motors)

Famous racer Campanelli (10) leading the pack through the curves on his 250-cc Benelli during a road race in Italy. (Cosmopolitan Motors)

the States you start a motocross with a live engine in gear and ready to go. In Japan you first warm up the engine, then on the crossed-flag signal kill it, and when the flag drops you kick-start and go. The start is the side-by-side kind used here. I was using either a 250-cc or 350-cc Yamaha.

"As for speed tracks, most of them are clay-surfaced, and it's similar to a scramble, without a jump. It's eighteen laps for the 250-cc class, and twenty-five laps for the open. This is

100

In a hard lean at high speed, Ed Moran (4 painted backward) on a three-cylinder Kawasaki road racer laps another competitor at Virginia Raceway in Danville, 1970. (*Kawasaki Motors*)

where you often see a smaller machine outrun the bigs—I often lapped a 350 with my 250.

"The thing you learn quickly is to watch everything, and at the same time listen to the sound of your bike. Mental attitude is important—you keep going in spite of being tired, bruised, and your kidneys killing you. Our common trouble was fouled plugs and wet coils. No matter how we wrapped the coil in plastic and tape, it would get wet.

101

Racing in Japan in motocross, scrambles, and speed track events, James Cooke of Valley Stream, New York, is seen in action on a Yamaha.

Sometimes one bike can stop a whole motocross. James Cooke is somewhere in the center. No one was hurt!

Jim Rice powers his BSA 650 twin to victory at the Houston Astrodome TT Race, February 6, 1970. (BSA Motorcycles)

"Advice? Find someone who can tell you what to do. Ride on dirt and see how you like it. It's a lot different from riding on pavement, a lot different. It's all a matter of learning when to do what—when to hit the brakes, the gas, or both. Otherwise, good luck."

Dirt track racing is another popular event that draws enthusiasts to watch riders tearing around an oval at highest possible speeds. Interestingly, these machines do not have any brakes front or rear because experience has taught the racers that you can get around a corner faster by sliding than by braking.

Skill is needed for any kind of competition riding, but one of the greatest tests of skill is to be found in the "English Trials" riding. There the contestants must ride their specially prepared machines over rocks and fallen trees, through brooks, streams, and mudholes, and any other nearly impossible-to-negotiate terrain. Trials machines are not set up for speed but rather for pulling power at a nearly standstill pace, high ground clearance, and short turning radius. Points are deducted from a rider's score when his foot touches the ground for any reason, if he rides out of the boundaries, if he comes to a stop, or if the engine stalls.

Faced with this variety of competitive opportunities, the would-be racer has only this question in mind: Where shall I try my hand first?

6 Maintenance and Troubleshooting

As you become familiar with your motorcycle, you realize how important it is to check the various parts from time to time. This routine checking is the one factor that will keep your bike from developing unexpected trouble on the road.

It's not difficult to maintain your machine in top shape. You don't need more than the average set of tools and the checklist in your owner's manual. In instances where special testing or overhaul equipment is mentioned, the work should be left to experienced service technicians at your dealer's shop.

When it comes to lubricating moving mechanical parts, no one can deny the value of oil and grease. If the wheels are to turn freely, the hubs need grease around the bearings—a job that needs to be done about every 10,000 miles. The shock absorbers also need oil replenishment if they are to give you a smooth ride. Wheel bearings and shock-absorber jobs are best handled by your dealer.

What you yourself should regularly check (once a week) is the oil level in the crankcase (if you have a four-stroke engine) or the oil in the gearbox (if you have a two-stroker).

About once a month check the condition of the chain to make sure it is not dry and caked with dirt. Simply dip a brush into some engine oil and run this over the full length of the chain, then wipe off all the drippings.

About twice a year apply a little oil to the insides of the speedometer cable housing and also to the throttle, clutch, and brake cable housings.

If your machine is equipped with a magneto system, you won't have to worry about the condition of the battery. If you have a battery and coil system, then the condition of the battery is important indeed.

Batteries, whether 6-volt or 12-volt types, are installed by the dealer after being given the correct charge. This means that the only thing you need to check is the electrolyte level in each cell. Once every two weeks unscrew the cell caps and, if necessary, add distilled water so that the plates inside the cell are submerged. Do not overfill. In very warm weather battery refilling may be necessary more often than in cold weather.

Neatness pays off where batteries are concerned. Use a special battery filler sold inexpensively in auto parts supply stores, and try not to spill the distilled water all over the battery. If you do mess up the job, be sure to wipe the battery dry before replacing the cell caps.

A weak battery is often the cause of hard starting, summer or winter. The spark needed to fire up an engine must be a good spark, and a weak battery just will not produce it. One simple way of quickly checking the condition of the battery is to switch on the headlight or sound the horn. The light should be bright, and the horn should sound healthy. During the winter months many riders remove the battery from the machine and store it indoors and also recharge it periodically with an inexpensive low-output "trickle" charger. When spring comes, they will have a battery in excellent shape. Others simply visit the garage once a week and start up the engine, run it for a while to charge the battery, and let it go at that.

But the quick check of switching on the light and sounding the horn could be deceptive; if any wire in the ignition system

No matter what the bike, sooner or later it must be serviced. Here two young enthusiasts learn about the simple musts from an experienced technician.

is loose at its connection or corroded, the energy from the battery simply won't get to where it's needed. So anytime you check the battery, also check the wires and their connections.

Whether you have a mag or battery system, make it a point to know the location of every fuse in the circuit, and then from time to time check the condition of the fuse holder itself.

If your machine suddenly becomes sluggish when you open the throttle or coughs and sputters when you're trying to start

Even on a minicycle the electrical connections must be checked. Most troubles can be traced to the wiring, spark plug, or breaker points.

up the engine, the trouble lies either in the ignition system or in the carburetor.

If you suspect ignition, disconnect the spark plug wire, get the plug out, and inspect the condition of the gap and the kind of carbon deposits around it. If it's black and sooty, your fuel mixture is too rich and is fouling the plug gap. The plug should be a dry gray kind, and the gap clearance should be as recommended by the book.

If you find the plug in good condition, check the breaker points. They may not be opening fully or opening too far, or they may be actually burned away. Any of these conditions will give you poor performance.

If you suspect carburetion, first check the gas tank, then the fuel shutoff valve, then the filter (if any). Finally, check whether or not the throttle is actually opening when you twist the grip. Also remember that a plugged-up air vent in the gas tank cap can create a vacuum and thus affect the running of the engine.

Another part of your routine checking or maintenance has to do with having a correctly tensioned chain. (Your tool kit should contain spare chain links.) Place your finger at midpoint of the upper stretch of the chain and press downward. If the slack is more than an inch, loosen the rear-wheel axle bolts and by turning the adjusters move the wheel backward to tension the chain properly. The slack should be about a half inch down—a total play of one inch. Tighten the bolts, and then check the rear wheel for alignment. If you do not move the rear wheel backward evenly on both sides, you'll have an out-of-line wheel, which will affect the handling of the bike. Checking the tension of the chain must be done with the bike off its center stand and with a rider seated. Wheel alignment can be done with the bike on the center stand.

Check the pressure in the tires once each week. Your man-

An improperly tensioned chain will cause trouble in the long run. Chain tension adjusters are located at the ends of the rear fork. After making an adjustment, be sure to tighten the locknuts and the main bolts.

ual will tell you which is the best pressure for solo riding and for two-up. Soft tires cause a motorcycle to veer erratically in a curve, refusing to keep to a straight line, while hard tires create too much bounce. For average riding 20 psi (pounds per square inch) for the front and about 25 psi for the rear are normal pressure.

The moment you start rolling out of your driveway or away from the curb, make it a point to check the action of both brakes. If either the front or the rear brake action feels soft, make the simple adjustments before you ride out into traffic. After you adjust the brakes—usually done by taking up the

Break cable to front wheel brake on this Jawa has convenient adjusting nut. After making adjustment, spin the wheel to make sure brake is not dragging.

M. V. Agusta rear brake is by rod, with convenient adjusting nut.

Clutch lever needs slight free play at the hinge. As fingers pull up the slack, a ⅛-inch gap is correct.

slack in the front cable and a few turns of the wing nut on the rear rod—spin each wheel to see if it turns freely. There should be no dragging or binding.

Since the clutch is directly responsible for transferring engine power to the rear wheel, you should make sure the clutch is properly adjusted on your bike. If it's not, you'll be damaging the clutch itself, and even the gears.

Clutch cable slack can be taken up at the clutch lever on the handlebar. This is a simple operation and is always explained in the manual. On some models you'll be able to see the clutch rod where it enters the clutch housing itself, and at this point the lever may also require a certain adjustment. Both adjustments, cable and rod, are simple and easy to do and should be part of your routine maintenance.

If you value the appearance of your motorcycle and are proud of it, as so many riders are, then dust on its polished paint surfaces and caked oil around the engine will bother you enough to give everything a periodic cleaning. Some riders wipe off dirt after every ride, others do it once a week, others once a month. How often you clean your bike shows how much you care for it.

This practice of routine checks and maintenance will work for you in the long run. It's the factory-trained motorcycle mechanics who say: Fifty percent of all problems can be eliminated if the machine receives routine care and maintenance!

Every owner's manual for the particular model motorcycle contains a troubleshooting chart which tells what to do when the engine starts to give you problems.

The usual troubleshooting chart is divided into three columns: TROUBLE—POSSIBLE CAUSE—REMEDY. Some charts are no more than brief outlines, while others cover many pages in the manual and explain all points in detail.

While the approach to troubleshooting is the same in nearly all cases, different engine and ignition configurations may require slightly different methods. For this reason a troubleshooting chart for all motorcycles is impossible in this book. The following, however, will provide you with a general understanding of what to do under the listed conditions.

One of the simplest forms of TROUBLE is that the engine cannot be started. If you begin to look for the POSSIBLE CAUSE, you may find no spark at the points or at the plug, or you may find an irregular spark, or you may find that you cannot flood the carb. The REMEDY then may be in one or in a combination of conditions, such as incorrect gap, blown fuse, empty fuel tank, closed-off fuel valve, or even a clogged air vent in the gas tank cap.

Now let's assume that the engine has been started but that the TROUBLE is poor performance. The engine may be misfiring, pinging, coughing, and each of these symptoms is a clue to POSSIBLE CAUSES, such as overheating, temporary short circuit, lean mixture, burned breaker points, or incorrect gap. And the REMEDY may be found in changing the spark plug to the right type, tracing for a loose wire connection and checking the battery terminal connections, checking the carb settings, replacing the breaker points, or adjusting the gap.

Whenever your machine misbehaves and you're sure that no parts inside the engine are broken, check for proper fuel delivery and the existence of a spark inside the cylinder. It is not uncommon for a rider to waste ten minutes or more kicking over his engine and then realize that he forgot to switch the ignition *on*. And many a rider has been forced to pull off the road and spend a great deal of time troubleshooting in the wrong direction, while all the time he had forgotten to fill the gas tank (or had forgotten to switch to his reserve fuel supply).

7 The Motorcycle's Family Tree

If you know what a Henderson, Pope, Merkel, Super-X, or Indian is, then either you are an old-time motorcycle rider or you have been reading the various magazines devoted to the sport of motorcycling. Those and other American models existed during the early development stage in motorcycling's history. Today they are only a reference for the millions of enthusiasts who are familiar with the current breed of bikes—mostly of European and Japanese manufacture.

After Gottlieb Daimler proved in 1885 (in Germany) that a gasoline engine could be mounted into a frame and the whole supported on two wheels—the real birth of the motorcycle!—people in different fields of manufacture turned their attention to the invention, and the struggle for improvement was on.

In England the Birmingham Small Arms Company, for example, was manufacturing small firearms and then began producing the BSA machines. Similarly, in Czechoslovakia the Janecek Arms Manufacturing Company merged with the German Wanderer Company and so, with the first two letters of each name, formed the now familiar Jawa range of bikes (the only manufacturer today producing regular street machines with automatic clutches). In Italy the same kind of sequence of events developed fine motorcycles for racing and for economical transportation.

In Japan, however, motorcycle production did not begin until quite late, and yet today their machines dominate the world market.

In the United States, oddly, the only name today is Harley-Davidson. Since the history of American motorcycling is unique, Emmett Moore, regional manager of Kawasaki Motors Corporation, who has long been associated with the motorcycling industry and who founded the Antique Motorcycle Club of America, agreed to provide the following historical highlights. In his words:

"In the spring of 1901 in Springfield, Massachusetts, Carl Oscar Hedstrom, the inventor and builder of the first *Indian* motorcycle, was about to demonstrate his motorized bicycle to a group of skeptics who, if the demonstration was a success, were to become Hedstrom's financial backers. The critical test was to be a run uphill on the steepest paved road in the area known as Cross Street Hill. Hedstrom's partner, George Hendee, was standing at the top of the hill, and when he gave the signal, Hedstrom started pedaling the motorized bicycle into popping activity. He made his dash uphill successfully, and thus began the motorcycle industry in the United States.

"Prior attempts by others to build commercially successful motorcycles were not sustained, and this left the *Indian* as the pioneer.

"The motorcycle was the natural outgrowth of the bicycling craze of the late 1890's and early 1900's. Then the development of a light, air-cooled engine made it possible to produce a machine that would eliminate pedaling. Between 1901 and through 1905 dozens of companies entered the motorcycle manufacturing field, and large numbers of machines were sold to people in all walks of life. These early motorcycles were essentially motorized bicycles, most of them with a direct belt or chain drive from the engine to the rear wheel, which neces-

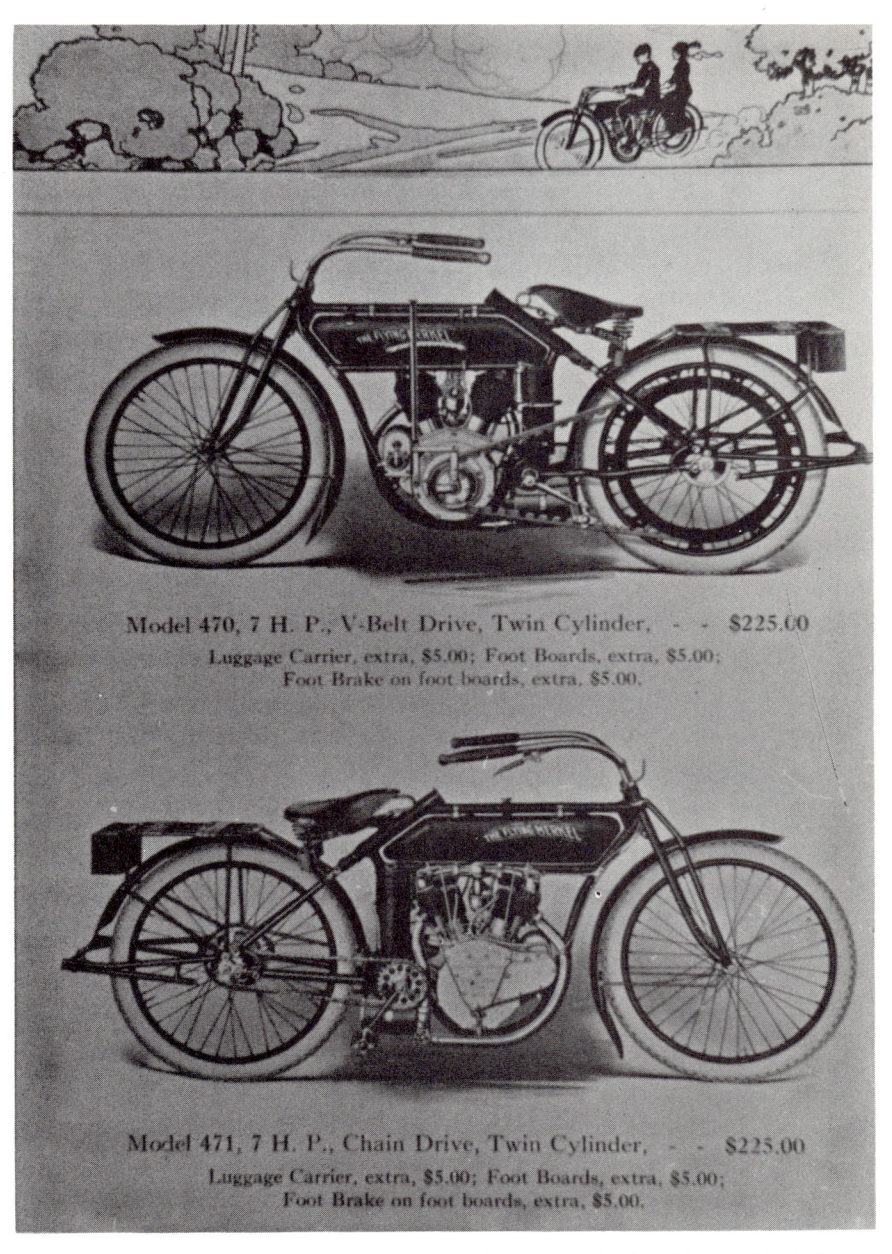

Model 470, 7 H. P., V-Belt Drive, Twin Cylinder, - - $225.00
Luggage Carrier, extra, $5.00; Foot Boards, extra, $5.00; Foot Brake on foot-boards, extra, $5.00.

Model 471, 7 H. P., Chain Drive, Twin Cylinder, - - $225.00
Luggage Carrier, extra, $5.00; Foot Boards, extra, $5.00; Foot Brake on foot boards, extra, $5.00.

A motorcycle ad during the 1910 era. The twin-cylinder Flying Merkel was available with belt or chain drive, with a 7-horsepower engine. A dandy motorcycle of its day. (*Emmett* Moore)

sitated pedaling the machine to start the engine and then a complete engine stoppage to come to a halt.

"Soon enough, however, manufacturers began to install clutches, and during this period of experimentation the engine was set in different positions, some on the handlebars, over the front wheel, over the rear wheel, and finally arriving at the now-standard position at the bottom of the V-shaped frame. The engines themselves were almost universally single-cylinder four-stroke types, with automatic intake valve operated by atmospheric pressure on the piston downstroke. Power was very low—one to two horsepower.

"In 1906 the motorcycle became heavier and more powerful. While the single-cylinder engine reigned supreme until about 1910, the twin-cylinder engine made its appearance. By 1907 some advanced makes, including Indian, Harley-Davidson, Excelsior, and Thor, were fitting two-speed gears, and all had some type of a spring front fork. During this period over one hundred manufacturers were producing motorcycles in America!

"Then in 1912 a small black bug appeared on the scene— the early-day Model-T Ford. Before this the motorcycle was aimed at the transportation market, but when the cheap and quite practical motorcar was made available, the market for motorcycles entered a rapid decline and by 1914 had virtually ceased to exist. By 1918 only about six manufacturers remained. Pope resumed bicycle production in Westfield, Massachusetts; Merkel today is Miami Cabinet Company; Thor entered the electrical appliance field; Ace was bought out by Indian; Henderson was bought out by Excelsior (Schwinn) in Chicago. By 1931 there remained only Indian and Harley-Davidson, and both were operating on a vastly reduced scale. At the time fewer than one hundred thousand motorcycles were registered in the United States.

"In 1950 Indian left the field, and so today Harley-Davidson is the only remaining motorcycle manufacturer in this country, but even they have joined the importers for their lightweight machines built in Italy.

"Following the end of World War II a new interest in motorcycling as a sport and hobby developed in the United States, and with no American-made machines to supply the demand, there began the present era of imported motorcycles, from England, Germany, Italy, Czechoslovakia, and then Japan.

"In the 1950's Honda (in Japan) began producing light two-stroke models designed for transportation purposes, and unlike their preceding production based on some British and American designs, these machines were new and original in concept. Yamaha, Suzuki, and Kawasaki followed Honda, all launching extensive advertising and promotional campaigns and selling hundreds of thousands of light machines across America. As the years went on, these manufacturers added larger models and increased their range to include off-road and competition machines. Within six years the motorcycle registration leaped into the millions!

"Perhaps one day United States industry will again become interested in motorcycle production. In the meantime an increasing segment of our young population is happily buzzing, burbling, and crackling across the countryside on well-designed, attractive, and reliable motorcycles in this New Age of Motorcycling."

Mr. Moore's sweep through history reminds us that as far back as 1904 the first hand twist-grip throttle was introduced; in May, 1907, the first Isle of Man T. T. (Tourist Trophy) race was run; in 1919 the first scooter appeared on the scene; in 1925 the first foot gearshift was used; and a world speed record of 134.6 miles per hour was set by Ernst Henne on a BMW in 1929, and the record stood for fourteen years!

In 1924 the American Motorcycle Association was organized for the purpose of having one organization which would set uniform rules and regulations to govern the sport of motorcycling over the entire United States and also sanction events for the charter clubs. At present the AMA has more than 125,000 members and 1,500 chartered clubs. It sanctions 500 professional events and 5,000 sportsman events each year, in which approximately 2,600 professional riders and 50,000 sportsman riders participate.

The Competition Congress of the AMA, made up of elected and appointed delegates, establishes the rules. One delegate is elected by the chartered clubs in a district to serve a two-year term. There are twenty-five AMA districts, and the districts are divided into three regions. A manufacturer of two-wheel motor vehicles, if he is a member of the AMA, may appoint two representatives to serve on the Competition Congress. The congress meets once each year in the fall to review all rules and make necessary revision, deletions, and additions, all of which have been submitted to the delegates by the AMA members and clubs. Riders who are interested in competition or a group wishing to form an AMA club may get particulars from any motorcycle dealer.

It was only natural that the increasing popularity of motorcycling has created a vast readership interest. Today the newsstands offer a variety of monthly magazines in which the latest trends, legislation, models, and racing reports and personalities are discussed. By reading about the sport, your enthusiasm will keep ticking, and at the same time you'll learn about the latest technical aspects—and even riding techniques.

Gene Romero rides his Triumph twin to victory at Sacramento, California, on September 13, clinching the 1970 Grand National Championship. (*Triumph Motorcycles*)

Index

Ace motorcycle, 118
Adjusters, chain, 109
Adjusting screws, carburetor, 32
Air cooling, 116
Air induction, 33
Air traffic, 70
Air vent, 109, 114
Alternator, 33
AMA (American Motorcycle Association, 120
Antique Motorcycle Club of America, 116
Ape-hangers, 62
Automatic oil feed system, 20, 22, 40
Automatic-type clutch, 13
Axle bolts, 109

Back seat, 92
Balance, 38, 43, 55, 84
Basic neutral, 48, 56
Battery, 33, 35, 106
Battery and coil ignition system, 33, 106
Bearings, 105
Bicycle, 9, 11, 27, 37, 116
Benelli motorcycle, 22
BMW motorcycle, 22, 27, 119
Boots, 64
Bore, 22
Bowl, carburetor, 32, 50
Brake linings, 50
Brakes, 27, 38, 56, 57, 86
Braking, 29, 49, 63, 70, 81, 89, 90
Breaker points, 33, 109
Break-in period, 22
BSA motorcycles, 53, 115

Cairo Public School, 53
Carburetor, 17, 20, 32, 50, 96, 109
Carburetor bowl, 40

Center stand, 38, 50, 62
Chain, 27, 79, 81, 105, 109
Chain links, spare, 36, 109
Charging battery, 106
Choke, 33, 41, 43, 50
Circles, 54, 68
Cleaning, 113
Clearance, breaker points, 109, 114
Clearance, spark plug gap, 109, 114
Close ratio, 46
Clothing, 75
Clubs, 120
Clutch, 13, 17, 25–27, 46, 51, 55, 56, 87, 91, 96, 112
Clutch control lever, 26, 43
Clutch plates, 26, 45
Competition Congress, 120
Competition machines, 16, 24, 33, 79, 119
Competition riders, 64, 93, 103
Competition ratio, 20
Compression stroke, 19, 20, 32, 41
Condenser, 33
Connections, 40, 43, 106, 114
Connecting rod, 17
Control, 52, 53, 56, 62, 71, 84, 86, 89, 90, 93, 96
Cooke, James, 96
Crankcase, 17, 22, 40
Crankshaft, 17, 27
Crash bars, 36
Critical Hours, The (film), 53
Curves, 56, 57
Czechoslovakia, 115, 119

Daimler, Gottlieb, 115
Dealers, 59, 65, 105, 120
Demonstration ride, 62
Directional light signals, 13

123

Dirt track, 93, 103
Discharging, battery, 36
Disengaged, clutch, 25, 26, 43, 45, 49
Displacement, engine, 22, 59, 60
Distilled water, 106
Downhill, 84
Dragster, 16
Driven gear, 27
Driver's license, 68
Driveshaft, 27
Dual-control trainer, 53

Electric starter, 13, 35, 38
Electrical energy, 33, 106, 107
Electrical spark, 19, 114
Electrolyte level, 33, 106
Emergency stopping, 52, 55
Enduro, 16, 29, 87, 93, 95
Engaged, clutch, 26
Engine, 16, 17, 26, 31, 79
Engine cooling, 43
England, 115, 119
English Trials, 103
Excelsior motorcycle, 118
Exhaust pipes, 31, 63
Exhaust stroke, 19, 20
Exhaust system, 31, 63, 92
Experimentation, 118
Eye protection, 64

Face shield, 64, 75
Fast stop, 50, 71
Faulty ignition, 41
Figure 8's, 50, 55, 68
Filters, 33, 109
Flat tire, 76, 77
Float, carburetor, 32
Fouled plugs, 101, 109
Four-stroke engine, 17, 22, 40, 105, 118
Frame, 31, 79, 118
Front brake lever, 27, 37, 43, 63
Fuel inlet, 33
Fuel level, 40, 114
Fuel mixture, 17, 20, 32
Fuel valve, 40, 49, 50, 93, 114
Fuse, 107, 114

Gap, spark plug, 43, 109, 114
Gearbox, 13, 17, 23–26, 35, 40, 71
Gearing, 16, 23, 24, 91, 96
Gearing down, 50, 52, 56
Gear shaft sprocket, 27, 79
Generator, 33
German Wanderer Company, 115
Germany, 119

Giro D'Italia, 95
Gloves, 38, 64
Goggles, 38, 64
Group riding, 75, 76

Handbrake, 38, 64
Handlebar, 26, 27, 62
Handling characteristics, 31, 62
Headlight, 35, 63, 67, 70, 72, 106
Heavyweight motorcycle, 16
Harley-Davidson motorcycle, 116, 118
Hedstrom, C. O., 116
Helmet, 38, 64
Hendee, George, 116
Henderson motorcycle, 115, 118
Henne, Ernst, 119
High gearing, 25
High seat, 62
Hill climber, 16
History, 115
Honda motorcycle, 53, 119
Horn, 33, 35, 63, 69, 70, 72, 76, 106
Horsepower, 12, 23
Hubs, 27

Idling speed, 32
Ignition, 41, 49, 50, 87, 93, 96, 109
Ignition system, 19, 33
Indian motorcycle, 115, 116, 118
Intake stroke, 19, 20, 22, 32
Instructional programs, 52
Insurance, 60
Intersections, 70, 74
ISDT (International Six Day Trials), 93
Isle of Man T. T., 119
Italy, 115, 119
Invisible Circle, The (film), 53

Janecek Arms Manufacturing Company, 115
Japan, 96, 115, 119
Jawa motorcycle, 22, 25, 53, 77, 115
Jawa Tatran motorcycle, 13
Jumping, 86, 87, 89

Kawasaki Motors Corporation, 116, 119
Kick starter, 35, 40, 41, 63
Kill button, 87
Knobbies, 87

Lambretta motorcycle, 13
Lean mixture, 32, 41
License, 17, 65, 67
Lightweight motorcycle, 13, 22, 71
Long-distance touring, 16

124

Loss of control, 74
Low gearing, 25
Lubrication, 105

Magneto ignition system, 33, 106
Maintenance, 43, 105, 113
Mediumweight motorcycle, 13
Merkel motorcycle, 115, 118
Mileage, 22
Minibike, 13, 59
Minicycle, 13, 59
Model T Ford, 118
Moore, Emmett, 116
Moped, 11, 22
Motocross, 16, 22, 29, 53, 79, 84, 87, 89, 93, 96, 100
Moto-Guzzi motorcycle, 27
Motorcycling magazines, 64, 120
Mufflers, 32
M. V. Agusta motorcycle, 27

Neutral, 25, 35, 40, 43, 45, 48, 49, 56
Night riding, 74

Off-the-road riding, 17, 92, 119
Oil level, 22, 40, 105
Oil pump, 20, 36
Oil tank, 40
Operator's permit, 65
Overhaul, 62, 105
Overheating, 114
Overstressing, 24, 48
Owner's Manual, 60, 77, 105, 112, 113

Parilla motorcycle, 95
Parking, 50, 68
Parts catalogue, 60
Passing, 67, 70–72
Patience, 68
Pedestrians, 93
Pegs, 63, 84, 93, 95
Performance, 16, 23, 24, 60, 79, 109, 114
Piston, 17, 20
Piston rings, 17
Pope motorcycle, 115, 118
Power, 46, 56
Power stroke, 17, 19, 20
Power output, 16, 22, 23
Power-to-weight ratio, 46, 71
Preignition, 49
Pressure, oil, 36
Primer, 33, 41

Quick start, 55, 56, 70
Quick stop, 55, 56, 70

Rain gear, 74
Reaction time, 70
Rear brake, 29, 37
Rear light, 70, 72
Rear sprocket, 17, 23, 27, 79
Rearview mirror, 36, 64, 72
Registering, 67, 68
Repair procedures, 62, 77
Reserve fuel, 114
Rich mixture, 32, 33, 41
Riding at night, 72, 74
Riding techniques, 70, 79, 81, 92, 96, 103, 120
Riding test, 17, 65, 68
Road racer, 16, 93
Road surface, 31, 62, 63, 70, 74
Rocker shift lever, 43
Rockers, 20
Rockwood, R. D., 52
Rottigni, Joseph, 93
Routine checking, 105, 109, 113

Saddle, 31
Safety, 64, 70
Sandpit practice, 79, 81, 84, 87
Scrambler, 16, 79, 93
Schwinn, 118
Scooter, 12, 22, 119
Separation, 70, 71, 76
Shifting, 25, 43, 46, 48, 51, 63, 71, 119
Shielding, exhaust pipe, 63
Shifting down, 50, 52, 56
Shock absorbing (suspension) system, 31, 62, 63, 105
Shop manual, 60
Shutting off engine, 50, 87
Sidecar, 16
Signaling, 67, 70–72, 92
Skidding, 72
Skill, 70, 79
Sliding, 56, 83, 103
Solo, 38, 75
Spark arrester, 92
Spark plug, 17, 32, 33, 106
Speed, 53, 54, 70, 71, 76, 86, 87
Speedometer, 35, 48, 106
Spin-around, 84
Sport regulations, 120
Sprockets, 79
Stalling, 46, 49, 55, 56, 87
Starting, 22, 33, 38, 40, 62, 63, 106, 113
Stoplight, 35, 63, 72
Stopping power, 38
Street bike, 16, 23, 29, 59, 79
Stroke, 22

125

Sunglasses, 72
Super-X motorcycle, 115
Suzuki motorcycle, 36, 119
Swerving, 81, 83
Swing-arm, 31
Switches, 35

Tachometer, 35, 48, 96
Tailgating, 70
Taillight, 35, 63
Tank, 32, 109, 114
Techniques, 70, 79, 81, 92, 96, 103, 120
Thor motorcycle, 118
Throttle, 32, 38, 41, 43, 46, 55, 119
Tickler, 33, 41
Tight circles, 50
Tight quarters, 50, 56
Tire irons, 77
Tire pressure, 29, 31, 78, 109
Tire pump, 36, 77
Tires, 17, 29, 31, 76, 77, 81, 96
Tools, 36, 60, 77, 105, 109
Torque, 26
Traffic, 62, 67, 69, 70, 71, 76, 81, 110
Trail bike, 16
Trail riding, 92
Trials, 16
Trickle charger, 106
Troubleshooting, 43, 77, 105–7, 113

Tube valve, 77
Tube patching kit, 36, 77
Tuned engine, 31
Tuning requirements, 32
Two-stroke engine, 20, 40, 105

Uphill, 86, 116
United States, 116, 118, 119, 120

Valve clearances, 22
Valve guides, 20
Valves, 20, 22
Venturi tube, 32
Vespa motorcycle, 13
Voltages, 33, 106

Warm weather, 41
Warranty, 60
Water temperature indicator, 36
Weather conditions, 31, 36, 41, 64, 72, 74
Wet coils, 101
Wheel alignment, 109
Wheelie, 90, 91
Wheels, 79, 105
Weight, 13, 16, 46, 60, 71
Windshield, 36
Winding out, 56, 71
Written test, 65, 68

Yamaha motorcycle, 22, 52, 53, 100, 119

The *HERE IS YOUR HOBBY* Series

FISHING
by WILLIAM MOORE

ARCHERY
by BERNHARD A. ROTH

SCIENCE EQUIPMENT
by WILLIAM MOORE

MAGIC
by BYRON WELS

HUNTING
by DION HENDERSON

DOLL COLLECTING
by HELEN YOUNG

CAR CUSTOMIZING
edited by HENRY GREGOR FELSEN

AMATEUR RADIO
by BYRON WELS

INDIAN DANCING AND COSTUMES
by WILLIAM K. POWERS

SLOT CAR RACING
by BOB BRAVERMAN and BILL NEUMANN

SKIING
by WILLIAM O. FOSS

STAMP COLLECTING
by FRANK CETIN

MODEL CAR BUILDING
by BILL NEUMANN

SNOWMOBILING
by JAMES JOSEPH

The Author

CHARLES YERKOW has been owner of three motorcycles at one time, has flown open-cockpit airplanes, and has taught judo at Queens College, but nevertheless has spent most of his waking hours at a typewriter. After an education in American and European schools, Mr. Yerkow began his writing career by specializing in aviation. Since then he has broadened his field into writing fiction for numerous magazines and nonfiction about a variety of technical and semitechnical subjects. Mr. Yerkow, a native New Yorker, lives in Beechhurst, New York.